HOTSPOTS
CROAT
DALMATIAN COAST

C000018509

Written by Plava Ponistra
Original photography by Plava Ponistra
Front cover photography by Grant Rooney/Thomas Cook Publishing
Series design based on an original concept by Studio 183 Limited

Produced by Cambridge Publishing Management Limited
Project Editor: Rosalind Munro
Layout: Natalie White
Maps: PC Graphics

Published by Thomas Cook Publishing
A division of Thomas Cook Tour Operations Limited
Company Registration No. 1450464 England
PO Box 227, Unit 18, Coningsby Road
Peterborough PE3 8SB, United Kingdom
email: books@thomascook.com
www.thomascookpublishing.com
+ 44 (0) 1733 416477

ISBN: 978-1-84157-760-9

First edition © 2007 Thomas Cook Publishing
Text © 2007 Thomas Cook Publishing
Maps © 2007 Thomas Cook Publishing
Project Editor: Diane Ashmore
Production/DTP: Steven Collins

Printed and bound in Spain by GraphyCems

CONTENTS

WHAT'S IN YOUR GUIDEBOOK?

Independent authors Impartial up-to-date information from our travel experts who meticulously source local knowledge.

Experience Thomas Cook's 165 years in the travel industry and guidebook publishing enriches every word with expertise you can trust.

Travel know-how Contributions by thousands of staff around the globe, each one living and breathing travel.

Editors Travel-publishing professionals, pulling everything together to craft a perfect blend of words, pictures, maps and design.

You, the traveller We deliver a practical, no-nonsense approach to information, geared to how you really use it.

● *Dubrovnik's magnificent city walls*

INTRODUCTION
Getting to know the Dalmatian coast

Dalmatian Coast

Legend:
- ○ City
- ○ Large Town
- ○ Small Town
- POI
- Motorway
- Main Road
- Minor Road
- ✈ Airport
- Railway

0 — 60 km
0 — 30 miles

N

Adriatic Sea

Ilovik
Pag
Pag Town
Zaton
Zadar
Park Prirode Telaščica
Dugi Otok
Park Prirode Paklenica
Gospić
E71
Bosansko Grahovo
Park Prirode Vransko Jezero
Nacionalni Park Krka
E65
Nacionalni Park Kornati
Šibenik
Zlarin
CROATIA
E71
Split
Trogir
Brač
Fortica Spanjola
Hvar Town
Vis
Vrboska
Hvar
Korčula
Last...

DALMATIA

Dalmatian Coast

Tuzla

BOSNIA-HERZEGOVINA

761
Jajce

Zenica

Bugojno

Vlasenica

.ivno

Sarajevo

Jablanica
Konjic

Goražde

Makarska

E65

Mostar

E762

Pelješac
eninsula

E73

Ploče

Orebić

Korčula
own

Ston

Slano

MONTENEGRO

nalni Park
Mljet

Mljet

Nikšić

Lopud

DUBROVNIK

E762

Cavtat

Dubrovnik ✈

Podgorica

Tivat

7

Getting to know the Dalmatian coast

The Dalmatian coast has been a popular destination for centuries, not just for tourists but also for settlers and conquerors – and it's no wonder. The region boasts an astonishing assortment of islands, a pristine sea, and unparalleled natural beauty. The Romans, Slavs, Venetians, Austro-Hungarians, French and Italians have all been here at one time or another, and their influence has left a mark on the region that remains to this day. This diverse assemblage has made Dalmatia home to some of the traditions that Croatians hold most dear. From the lace produced on Pag island to the dance performed on Korčula to *a capella* singing near Split, you can sample the things that make this region so rich in heritage and tradition.

Dalmatia also stands out linguistically, as the Croatian spoken here is slightly different from the language spoken inland. It is perhaps a Dalmatian word that best describes the lifestyle you can expect to experience during your visit to the region. *Fjaka* describes a good-natured, easy-going, stress-free approach to life, of which the Dalmatians are master practitioners. Yes, life is good. If a group of locals spontaneously bursts into song on the street, simply take it as evidence of this fact.

Dalmatians are proud of their delicious food, their wine and their beautiful surroundings. And they are proud of their cities. Split is the largest and most important city in the region. Zadar is an up-and-coming city with a fascinating collection of architectural highlights. Šibenik is a small town that can surprise you with the beauty of its surroundings, both natural and man-made. Dubrovnik's old city is a UNESCO-protected gem right on the sea. All of these cities offer access to some of Croatia's islands, each one of which has its own charms to discover, including unspoiled natural beauty, secluded beaches and fascinating history. They can all be reached using the excellent boat and ferry system in the area, or you can rent a boat and create your own itinerary.

A relaxing pace that is sure to recharge your batteries, a rich cultural and historical tradition to explore, delectable food and drink, not to mention some truly wild nightlife: all of these elements combine to make the Dalmatian coast an ideal place to spend a holiday. When you leave, you may feel as if you're stepping back into the 'real world' after a much-needed break from reality. Feel free to take a bit of the *fjaka* philosophy home with you.

⬤ *Sunset over the islands*

THE BEST OF THE DALMATIAN COAST

Enthusiastic travellers from around the world keep coming back to the pure waters and immaculate beaches of Croatia's coast. This exquisite scenery serves as the backdrop for any visitor's perfect holiday. Lounging on the beach may form part of your itinerary, but there are plenty of events and sights that are absolutely not to be missed.

TOP 10 ATTRACTIONS

- **Zadar: Crkva sv Donatus (St Donat's Church)**
  This pre-Romanesque church was founded in the 9th century and stands as the definitive symbol of Zadar (see page 22).

- **Zadar: Sea Organ (Morske orgulje)**
  A pipe organ that is played by the whims of the wind and sea, it is a creation unique to the city (see page 24).

- **Zadar: musical evenings in St Donat's**
  The excellent acoustics of this church are an advantage during this international festival of Medieval and Renaissance music (see page 106).

- **Šibenik: Nacionalni park Kornati (Kornati National Park)**
  In Kornati, 147 islands, reefs and islets form the largest and most beautiful archipelago in the Adriatic (see page 73).

- **Šibenik: Katedrala sv Jakova (The Cathedral of St James)**
  This outstanding cathedral is one of Croatia's most important buildings, dating from the 15th and 16th centuries (see page 29).

- **Split: Dioklecijanova palača (Diocletian's Palace)**
  One of the most important architectural attractions in Europe, this massive palace stands as the centrepiece of old Split and the core of the modern city (see page 37).

- **Biševo Island: Modra špilja (Blue Grotto), near Vis**
  The noon sun is reflected up from the white sand of the sea floor, creating an enchanting blue light inside the cave (see page 85).

- **Dubrovnik: Dubrovačke ljetne igre (Summer Festival)**
  The most celebrated cultural event in Croatia, featuring international artists in music, art, theatre and dance (see page 108).

- **Dubrovnik: Gradske zidine (City Walls)**
  The magnificent 13th-century walls of Dubrovnik's old city are almost perfectly preserved, extending 2 km (1 mile) to entirely surround the historic centre (see page 60).

- **Mljet Island: Nacionalni park Mljet (Mljet National Park)**
  Shrouded in legend and mystery, this densely forested island offers a wealth of natural beauty to explore (see page 89).

◗ *Split Summer Festival*

SYMBOLS KEY

The following symbols are used throughout this book:

a address   **t** telephone   **f** fax   **e** email   **w** website address
c opening times   **N** public transport connections   **i** important

The following symbols are used on the maps:

i information office		**O** city	
X post office		**O** large town	
shopping		○ small town	
airport		■ poi (point of interest)	
+ hospital		=== motorway	
police station		— main road	
bus station		— minor road	
railway station		— railway	
church			
1 numbers denote featured cafés, restaurants & evening venues			

RESTAURANT CATEGORIES

The symbol after the name of each restaurant listed in this guide indicates the price of a typical three-course meal without drinks for one person:

£ under €20   ££ €20–€40   £££ over €40

▶ *The Peristil, entrance to the palace and cathedral in Split*

RESORTS
Places under the sun

Pag

Visitors to Pag arriving from the mainland by ferry might be surprised to find themselves confronted with a landscape more suggestive of the moon than an Adriatic island. This is part of the charm of the island, as it possesses several oddities that make it a unique place to visit, one of which is the shape of the island itself. The slender fingers protruding from the island create little bays of still water, water that is extremely high in salt content. With all that salt in the air, vegetation has a hard time surviving on the island, so the principal agricultural activity has been sheep farming. The salty diet of the animals and the aromatic herbs they dine on give a distinctive flavour to their meat and to their milk, which is used to make one of the island's most sought-after products, Pag cheese. Authentic Pag cheese is hard, with a sharp flavour reminiscent of Parmesan. The women of Pag are known for their skill in producing another of Pag's treasured items, Pag lace, coveted around the world.

After you've sampled the local wares, it's time to indulge in the activity that really put Pag in the spotlight: decadent partying. This can be easily accomplished in the most populated town on the island, Novalja. Just a couple of kilometres away, the beach at Zrće awaits, which many have taken to referring to as the 'Croatian Ibiza'. Several clubs and bars, along with some of Zagreb's most popular nightlife spots (which decamp here in the summer), have staked their claim on this beach. Partying seems to reign as the number one activity on the island, but Pag's 270 km (168 miles) of coastline present plenty of opportunities to seek refuge. After you've chosen the perfect secluded spot from which to witness the sun going down on the still waters of the sea, you'll be glad you took the time to explore one of Croatia's most popular destinations.

BEACHES

Pag Bay

The bay in Pag Town goes on and on, creating an extremely long, sandy beach where you'll certainly have enough room to spread out your towel.

🔺 A view of Pag beach and town on its isthmus

Ručica
A beautiful, white-pebble beach complete with a view of the Velebit Mountains on the mainland makes this one of the best swimming spots on Pag. To get there, turn left at the wooden sign before the village of Metajna. Keep walking and follow the road to the end.

PAŠKI SIR – PAG CHEESE
The barren spaces of the island of Pag, in the very northern reaches of Dalmatia, produce special characteristics in the produce that arrives from it. The dry and rocky hills here provide a landscape on which sheep can be let loose. What little vegetation (including hardy medicinal herbs) they can manage to find is caressed by the sturdy *bora* (a brisk northern wind) which carries with it salt from the surrounding seas. This high sodium diet imparts special flavours to the hard, salty and absolutely glorious cheese that is made from their milk and then coated in olive oil whilst it ripens.

THINGS TO SEE & DO

Crkva sv Marije (Church of St Mary)
Dalmatian architectural superstar Juraj Dalmatinac was responsible for this magnificent construction in Pag Town. The church fits in perfectly with the unembellished beauty of the buildings surrounding it and the square in which it resides.
ⓐ Trg Petra Krešimira IV 🕑 09.00–12.00 & 17.00–19.00 May–Sept; for services only, Oct–Apr

Muzej paške čipke (Pag Lace Museum)
A comprehensive survey of the island's most famous handicraft.
ⓐ Kralja Zvonimira 🕑 open June–Aug, closed Sept–May

PAŠKA ČIPKA – PAG LACE

The tradition of making lace is so well regarded on the island of Pag that there is now a lace-making school well established in the town of the same name – a resurrection of a former school that had run since the turn of the 20th century. It was back in this time that Pag lace had become famous in its own right and was decorating the homes of the royalty of Europe. Previously, the local industry had had its work presented as Greek, Austrian or Italian on the world markets. The lace – 50 cm (20 in) in diameter – consists of a different pattern for each piece, never to be exactly repeated. The painstaking creation of the intricate circular patterns is carried out by the women of the town. When much of the younger population began to leave the island to find work elsewhere, it was realised that the tradition and skills could well be lost – thus the reawakening of the school.

Paška solana (Pag Salt Factory)

The production of salt has been one of Pag's staple industries for years. It's done the old-fashioned way, letting sea water evaporate and then gathering the residue. Tours of the salt factory can be arranged through the Pag tourist board. Just make sure you give them one day's notice.

ⓐ Svilno ⓣ 023 61 13 01

Talijanova buža (Italian Hole)

Dubbed the 'Italian hole' after the Romans who constructed this ancient water-delivery system in the 1st century, this is one of the most interesting sights on the island. The entrance is in the Novalja town museum.
ⓐ Zvonimir, Novalja ⓒ 09.00–19.00 Mon–Sun (summer)

TAKING A BREAK

Bars & cafés

Jež £ This is the prime vantage point on the town's main square. Enjoy a coffee while watching people making their way to the beach or revellers preparing for the nightly sojourn to Zrće. ⓐ Gajac A-10 ⓣ 098 75 08 94 ⓒ 06.00–24.00 (summer); closed winter

Restaurants

Konoba 85 ££ A truly classy *konoba* (an old-fashioned, traditional restaurant) with a spacious, roofed terrace and lovely décor, this is one of the best places in town to enjoy traditional Dalmatian cuisine served by an attentive and polite staff. If you don't feel like eating outside, retreat to the equally spacious interior. ⓐ Josipa Kunkere 4, Novalja ⓣ 053 66 36 80 ⓒ 10.00–24.00

Restoran Riva ££ The seafood and traditional Dalmatian fare are both excellent, as well as the views: one of the harbour just a short distance from the restaurant and the other of the open kitchen where the food is prepared. ⓐ Primorska b1, Novalja ⓣ 053 66 19 65 ⓦ www.restaurant-riva.com ⓒ 10.00–24.00 (summer); closed winter

Sidro ££ A nicely decorated, spacious interior will get you in just the right mood to enjoy the assortment of quality meals offered up by this combination restaurant and hotel. This is your opportunity to try that famous Pag lamb, or you can choose from their fabulous seafood menu.
ⓐ Braničevica, Gajac ⓣ 053 68 47 23 ⓦ www.bistro-sidro.com ⓒ 11.00–23.00 (summer); closed winter

Boškinac £££ The owner of Beach Bar Kalypso (see below) pulled out all the stops and opened the best restaurant on Pag. Expect a classy, slow-food experience, with traditional cooking methods and natural ingredients. ⓐ Skopljanska 20, Novalja ⓣ 053 66 35 00 ⓦ www.boskinac.com ⓛ 12.00–24.00 (summer); closed Jan

AFTER DARK

Aquarius £££ The best club in Zagreb has an equally good space on Pag. Come for the beach party, eat and drink, indulge in some ice cream, and even work out in the aerobics club during the day. A pool in the bar area awaits should you happen to work up a sweat doing all that dancing. What more could you ask for? ⓐ Zrće beach, Novalja ⓛ 24 hours (summer); closed winter

Beach Bar Kalypso £££ A pumping beach party complete with games like beach volleyball and badminton, food, internet access and drinks to keep you hydrated during it all. This one stays open until the sun comes up. ⓐ Zrće beach, Novalja ⓛ 24 hours (summer); closed winter

Beach Bar Papaya £££ Another Zagreb club makes its presence known on the beaches of Zrće, with excellent results. Fitted out with swimming pools, a water slide and jacuzzi, the crowd starts showing up in the late afternoon for drink promotions and foam parties. At 20.00, the music kicks up again and just keeps going. ⓐ Zrće beach, Novalja ⓦ www.papaya.com.hr ⓛ 24 hours (summer); closed winter

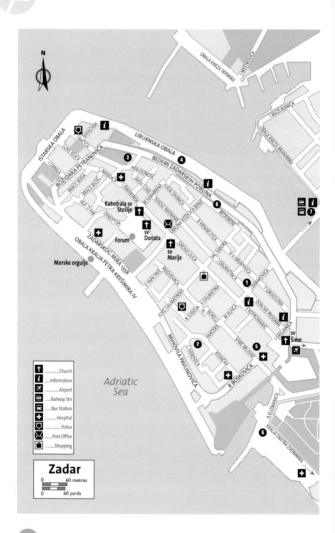

Zadar

0 — 60 metres
0 — 60 yards

Adriatic Sea

Church
Information
Airport
Railway Stn
Bus Station
Hospital
Police
Post Office
Shopping

Zadar

Zadar is the ideal spot for a family holiday. It is known as one of the safest cities on the Croatian coast and has that relaxed atmosphere so characteristic of the region. There could be few better places in which to while the day away, drinking coffee and people-watching. This 2,000-year-old city boasts a rich historical tradition, primarily evidenced by the splendidly preserved architecture to be seen all around. Much of the centre is composed of narrow medieval streets where traffic is banned. There are also some lovely 19th-century buildings on the south side of town. When you have strolled the lanes of ages past and discovered the well-hidden parks and gardens, venture out to the area surrounding Zadar for sunbathing and relaxing on the beach.

BEACHES

Kolovare

The main public beach is located east of the Old Town. The water is clean and makes for an acceptable place to have a dip. There are also plenty of restaurants and cafés in the area, some of which are open well into the night, making this a cool place to hang out, regardless of the time of day. You can even play table tennis under the shade of the trees near the beach.

Zaton

If you're in Zadar and want to hit a 'blue flag' beach, there's one about 16 km (10 miles) from the city in the village of Zaton. Once you're there, you'll see why it received the eco-label for quality. There is a whole range of services available, from a bar with a water slide to playgrounds for the kids and shops and restaurants. It also has disabled access. The beach itself is a pebbly, shallow lagoon surrounded by pine forest.

THINGS TO SEE & DO

Crkva sv Donata (St Donat's Church)

At the same time imposing and harmonious, this pre-Romanesque church was completed in the 9th century and stands as the best-preserved and most important construction of its kind in the region. Its original and unique form has gradually made it a symbol of the spirit of Dalmatia.

According to legend, St Donat's was founded by the Irish St Donat. The stone from the Roman forum (see below) came in very handy for the building of this church.

Inside, the church is bare and simple. It is no longer used for religious purposes, though concerts are held here from time to time during the summer months.

ⓐ Trg opatice Čike 1 🕒 July–Aug 09.00–21.00, Apr–June, Sept & Oct 09.00–13.00 & 16.00–20.00; closed winter ❶ Admission charge

Crkva sv Marije (St Mary's Church) and Stalna isložba crkvene umjetnosti (Museum of Church Art)

This 12th-century church has the oldest tower in Dalmatia. The Benedictine convent next door has an interesting museum, exhibiting various church treasures. These include some grisly relics, including the arm of St Isidore and St Mark's shoulder-blade, each contained in unusual caskets. Apart from these, there is some fascinating art in this museum. Creations from local gold- and silversmiths from the 8th through to the 18th centuries are presented in intimate fashion, creating a collection and ambience that is really exceptional.

ⓐ Šimuna Kožičića Benje 🕒 10.30–12.00 & 16.30–18.00 Mon–Sat; 10.00–12.30 Sun ❶ Admission charge

Crkva sv Šime (St Simeon's Church)

Built in the 16th and 17th centuries, this baroque church displays the reliquary of St Simeon, the saint/protector of the city who was reputed to have held the Christ Child in the Temple. The saint's silver-gilt

sarcophagus, which dominates the altar, was commissioned in 1377 by Queen Elizabeth of Hungary. It took 250 kg (550 lbs) of silver to fashion the relief panels which cover and line the casket. They show scenes from the saint's life and the history of the city. The interior is visible once a year when the coffin is opened on the saint's feast day (8th October).
ⓐ Trg Petra Zoranića 7 ⓣ 023 21 17 05 ⓛ 08.00–12.00 & 18.00–20.00 Mon–Sun, June–Sept

⬥ *Crkva sv Donata (St Donat's Church)*

Forum (City forum)

Zadar's Roman forum is the largest on the eastern side of the Adriatic. It was founded by the first emperor, Augustus, as recorded on two 3rd-century stone carvings on the site. The raised zone on the west side was a temple dedicated to Jupiter, Juno and Minerva. Off to one side stands the 'Pillar of Shame', where disorderly citizens were chained and derided. Apparently the shaming business was a popular one, as a second pillar was moved from the site and now stands near Three Wells Square. The historical significance of the forum is obvious, but the interesting thing about it is that it remains a living part of the city.

Katedrala sv Stošije (Cathedral of St Anastasia)

Built during the 12th and 13th centuries, St Anastasia's is the largest Romanesque cathedral in Dalmatia. A feature common to other Dalmatian churches is the belfry that stands separately from the rest of the church. The interior includes a stone ciborium over the high altar, an elaborately carved choir, frescoes and an Early Christian mosaic located in the sacristy. The interior of the church is attractive, but climb to the top of the bell tower to soak up the best view of the layout of Zadar, complete with terracotta roofs, gardens, mountains and sea.

🅐 Trg sv Stošije 2 🅣 023 25 17 08 🅛 08.00–13.00 & 17.00–18.00; closed Sun

Morske orgulje (Sea Organ)

Situated right on the quayside, a set of simple stone steps offers a perfect place to sit and enjoy one of Zadar's famous sunsets. Right under your seat, the world's first pipe organ to be played by the sea produces an ever-changing procession of whistled notes and chords. As the soothing sounds emanate from the 70-m (230-ft) organ, you can sit and appreciate the new centre for culture and leisure that this unique installation has created.

🅐 Obala kralja Petra Krešimira IV

⬥ *The tower of the City Hall in Zadar*

TAKING A BREAK

Bars & cafés

Lovre £ ❶ This café has the best location on the main square. The interior is actually a former church, but don't sit inside if you can enjoy the colourful and lively square instead. ⓐ Trg Narodni 1 ❶ 023 21 26 78 🕒 07.00–01.00

Trattoria Canzona £ ❷ A solid pizzeria carrying the same name as its sister restaurant in Zagreb. Visitors to either will tell you that it serves one of the best pizzas in town. ⓐ Stomorice 8 ❶ 023 21 20 81 🕒 10.00–23.00

Arsenal ££ ❸ Formerly a storehouse for materials used to service the fleet that protected the Venetian Republic's trade routes, Arsenal is now a centre for culture. Divided into five enormous sections, this place has it all: a time capsule showing the history (and future) of the city, a culture centre with regular exhibitions and performances, a market featuring local products, a lounge with drinks and food, and an information centre where you can find absolutely anything you need to know about the city. A must-see. ⓐ Trg tri bunara 1 ❶ 023 25 38 33 🌐 www.arsenalzadar.com 🕒 07.00–16.00 (summer); 07.00–15.00 (winter)

PRŠUT – SMOKED HAM

While other nations smoke ham and fight lawsuits for trying to pass it off as Parma, the Croats are more than happy to give their produce its own name and character – the latter apparently imparted by the process of drying it in the *bora* wind. This Dalmatian delicacy tends to be a little tougher and more robust in flavour than its Italian cousin. However, should you be able to get hold of the *pršut* from Posedarje (near Zadar), you won't be disappointed – it is tender and has a delicious flavour.

Maya Pub ££ ❹ This has a wood interior with a sculpture of Shiva on the wall. During the day, there's a lovely quayside terrace where you can watch the boats in the harbour. At night, a diverse mix of chilled-out dance music spins, or a popular Croatian band plays to an enthusiastic crowd. ⓐ Liburnska Obala 6 ❶ 023 25 17 16 ❷ 07.00–03.00

The Garden £££ ❺ Founded by UB40 drummer James Brown, The Garden is situated on the city walls and has an extremely comfy vibe, making it a great place to enjoy the superb view, have a drink and catch some rays. ⓐ Bedemi zadarskih pobuna ❶ 023 25 45 09 ❷ 10.00–01.00 May–Sept; closed winter

Restaurants
Na po ure £ ❻ This little *konoba* offers excellent value for money. The speciality of the house here is shark, but they also do meat and fish on the grill and a selection of other traditional Croatian dishes. ⓐ Špire Brusine 8 ❶ 023 31 20 04 ❷ 09.30–01.00

Foša ££ ❼ Named for the harbour, which it overlooks. The fish at this restaurant is renowned throughout the city for being exceptionally good. The terrace is perfect for a romantic evening out. ⓐ Kralja Dmitra Zvonimira 2 ❶ 023 31 44 21 ❷ 11.00–24.00

AFTER DARK

Gotham ££ ❽ A combination of café, cinema and wild party space, Gotham has become the prime party spot in Zadar, with regular live music and DJs spinning house, R&B and disco. ⓐ Marka Oreškovića 1 ❶ 023 20 02 89 ❷ 23.00–04.00

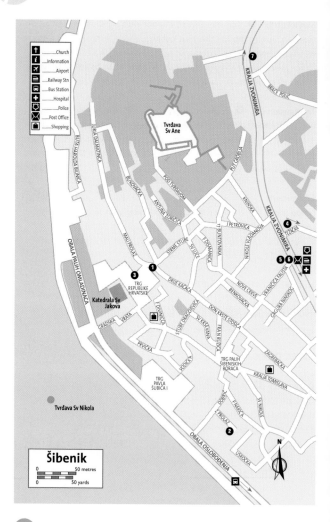

Key

- ✝ ......Church
- _i_ ......Information
- ✈ ......Airport
- ⬒ ......Railway Stn
- ⬓ ......Bus Station
- ✚ ......Hospital
- ⬙ ......Police
- ✉ ......Post Office
- ⬚ ......Shopping

Tvrdava Sv Ane

Katedrala Sv Jakova

Tvrdava Sv Nikola

TRG REPUBLIKE HRVATSKE

TRG PALIH ŠIBENSKIH BORACA

TRG PAVLA ŠUBIĆA I

Šibenik

0 — 50 metres
0 — 50 yards

Šibenik

Like so much of the Adriatic coast, the position of the current town of Šibenik was of strategic importance throughout much of history. It has the distinction of being the only city on the Adriatic coast originally founded by Croats, and is also known as the birthplace of Dražen Petrović, a household name in the world of Croatian sport, at one time the most talented European basketball player in the NBA. It is home to the remarkable Cathedral of St James, masterwork of transitional Gothic-Renaissance architect and sculptor Juraj Dalmatinac. There are two major national parks in the area that you can't afford to miss either: Kornati, with its hundreds of islands and reefs, and Krka, with its spectacular waterfalls and caves. Šibenik is a really engaging city, full of festivals and culture and the starting point for a visit to some of Croatia's most breathtaking destinations.

BEACHES

Jadrija
When the locals want to relax on the beach, they head to Srima peninsula and the excellent swimming of Jadrija beach. This is a favourite site for weekend homes; tourists also come to enjoy the beautiful public beach surrounded by pine forests. It is perfect for a day trip, but it might be even better if you can stop over in some of the privately owned accommodation offered in the area.

THINGS TO SEE & DO

Katedrala sv Jakova (Cathedral of St James)
Completed in 1555 after 105 years of construction, this UNESCO-protected cathedral is a perfect expression of the cultural fusion so characteristic of the region, combining the architectural styles of northern Italy and Tuscany. Although principally envisioned by

Dalmatinac, several architects participated in the project following the death of the master in 1473. This ambitious monument, constructed entirely of stone, presented special construction problems: this resulted in a unique design that documents the shift from Gothic to Renaissance architecture. Inside the cathedral are portraits from the time of its construction featuring 74 Šibenik citizens.

ⓐ Trg Republike Hrvatske ❶ 022 21 48 99 🕐 09.30–18.30 Mon–Sat, 13.00–18.30 Sun (summer); 09.30–12.00 & 16.00–18.00 Mon–Sat, 13.00–18.00 Sun (winter)

Tvrđava sv Nikola (Fortress of St Nicholas)

In the middle of the 16th century, the people of Šibenik were confronted with a problem: what to do about the Turks who kept trying to invade the city's port from the sea? Their answer was to build an island fortress to protect the sv Ante Strait. While no longer necessary for defensive purposes, the fortress makes a fascinating place to visit.

⬤ *The impressive Tvrđava sv Nikola, built to deter invaders*

TAKING A BREAK

Bars & cafés

Art Caffe-Gallery Madrigal ££ ❶ A combination bar and art gallery that features permanent exhibitions, book nights and meetings with some of Šibenik's intelligentsia, the ground floor of the Gogola Palace is one of the coolest places in town to grab a drink. The interior features painted Gothic beams that support the ceiling, lovingly restored by the owner of the café. Even the tables in the place are a special attraction, featuring signatures of famous folk from Šibenik. ⓐ Stube Jurja Čulinovića 3 ⓣ 091 211 09 62 ⓦ www.mediacaffe.net ⓛ 09.00–14.00 & 17.00–24.00 Mon–Thur, 09.00–14.00 & 17.00–01.00 Fri & Sat, 09.00–14.00 Sun

Indigo Bar ££ ❷ A hip, minimalist interior and excellent service make Indigo Bar the local favourite for coffee. ⓐ Trg Jurja Barakovića 4 ⓣ 091 789 21 87 ⓛ 08.00–01.00

Restaurants

Gradska vjeçnica ££ ❸ Smack bang in the centre of the Old Town, this classy restaurant enjoys the benefits of prime location on the ground floor of the Town Hall, which was erected between 1533 and 1546. The menu features modern fare inspired by traditional Dalmatian cuisine. They also have several vegetarian selections and other healthy options. ⓐ Trg Republike Hrvatske 1 ⓣ 022 21 36 05 ⓛ 08.00–24.00 (summer); 09.00–24.00 (winter)

Uzorita ££ ❹ A Šibenik favourite for over 100 years, this classy restaurant is the real deal. Almost the entire menu is composed of local favourites straight from the sea, and you can add a selection from the solid wine list or indulge in some homemade schnapps to round off your meal. If you have a hankering to crack open some of Šibenik's famed mussels, this place has its very own shell farm, so the freshness is guaranteed. ⓐ Bana Josipa Jelačića 58 ⓣ 022 21 36 60 ⓛ 11.00–24.00

Zlatna ribica ££ ❺ Another of Šibenik's favourites that has been at it for a very long time, this restaurant has a finely furnished space overlooking a beautiful bay located just out of town. The menu is full of the usual fish and meat specialities. One of the local Šibenik delicacies comes highly recommended: salted anchovies in olive oil. Live music on Friday and Saturday nights. ⓐ Krapanjskih Spužvara 46, Brodarica ⓣ 022 35 03 00 ⓦ www.zlatna-ribica.hr ⓛ 12.00–23.00

AFTER DARK

Aurora £££ ❻ Šibenik isn't exactly world famous for its nightlife, but the small town of Primošten 15 km (9 miles) from the city is home to one of the largest clubs in the Adriatic. Playground of celebrities and thousands of tourists every summer, the club has three levels, six bars, a chill-out room, a swimming pool, games and a pizzeria. There's also a full sit-down restaurant on site, making this your headquarters for a night out. ⓐ Kamenar ⓣ 098 66 85 02 ⓦ www.aurora.hr ⓛ 22.00–05.00 (summer); closed winter

Hacienda £££ ❼ The search for exciting nightlife will once again take you outside of the city of Šibenik, this time 10 km (6 miles) to Vodice and another of the most popular nightclubs in all of Croatia. The top international DJs spinning the hottest house records plus the superb interior have made this a magnet for clubbers. ⓐ Magistrala ⓣ 091 586 86 97 ⓦ www.hacienda.hr ⓛ 22.00–05.00 (summer); closed winter

Šibenik by night

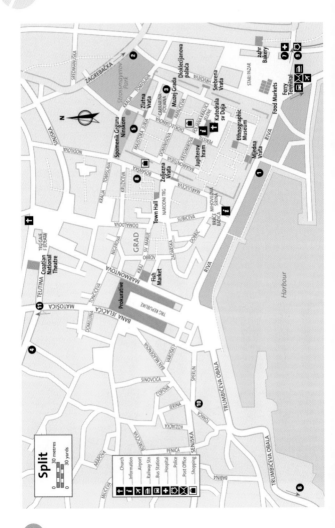

Split

The 3rd-century Roman Emperor Diocletian was known for his political reforms as well as for his relentless persecution of Christians. His enormous retirement palace formed the core of ancient Split, and today remains at the heart of the modern city, with shops, markets and even a Christian cathedral woven into the fabric of the original palace. The city eventually became the second-largest city in Croatia and an important cultural and economic centre for Dalmatia and the rest of the country. It is also a major travel hub for the region, with many ferry, train and bus routes passing through the city. This makes Split a great place in which to stop and recharge your batteries, before heading out again. One piece of advice: don't wear any Dinamo Zagreb gear, as the football fans in Split are loyal followers of Hajduk, who enjoy an intense rivalry with the Dinamo.

Discovering the city is an interesting experience of uncovering the new along with the old. There are the predictable modern additions to Split, such as an international airport, chemical plants, a university and many scientific institutions. However, the people of Split have had the foresight and wisdom to allow past and present to coexist, creating a fascinating fusion of ancient history and modern living that is a pleasure to explore.

BEACHES

Bačvice

During your travels, you might well notice small groups of guys and gals standing waist-deep in the water, keeping a small ball in the air and making dramatic, diving saves to keep it aloft. The game is called Picigin, and Split's beaches have seen some of the meanest Picigin playing in the world. A short, five-minute walk south of the train station will get you to Bačvice, a 'blue flag' (see page 53) beach and the perfect proving ground for your Picigin skills. Bačvice has a number of cafés lining the sandy beach where you can slake your thirst and prepare for the evening. Club Shakespeare is a popular nightspot right on the beach that features DJs and a whole lotta dancing.

◆ *Looking over the cathedral and port of Split*

Uvala Bene (Bene Cove)

A short bus ride to the northern side of the peninsula will get you to Bene Beach, Split's most popular family beach. Pine trees extend nearly to the waterfront, offering shade for picnics and relaxing. Let the kids go wild in the playground or take a ride on a pony. There's also a snack bar and tennis courts.

THINGS TO SEE & DO

Dioklecijanova palača (Diocletian's Palace)

Diocletian spared no expense in constructing his enormous palace, built in anticipation of his retirement from politics in 305. Commissioned in 293, the palace's construction required materials from all around the region, including white stone from the nearby island of Brač and columns and sphinxes all the way from Egypt. The immense structure was completed in ten years and is truly the definition of a 'living museum', as some 2,000 people reside in the 220 buildings contained in the palace's boundaries. There are three fortified gates in the western, northern and eastern walls, along with a smaller gate in the southern wall. This wall led from the servant's quarters to the sea. Krešimirova Street runs east to west and separated the servants' and soldiers' quarters from the temples and Diocletian's residence.

Jupiterov hram (Temple of Jupiter)

Only one of the three temples that formerly resided on the west side of the Peristyle (see page 39) remains today, although you can still see remnants of the other two. The Temple of Jupiter was Christianised, becoming a baptistry in the early Middle Ages.

Katedrala sv Duje (Cathedral of St Domnius)

Being a Christian was a dangerous business at the time of Emperor Diocletian's residency in Split. One of the most famous victims of his cruelty was Saint Domnius. Diocletian had him beheaded for

● *Children celebrating the Split Summer Festival*

attempting to spread Christianity throughout the region. Domnius's bones were placed in Diocletian's mausoleum within the palace and the entire structure converted into the Cathedral of St Domnius. Many historians maintain that St Domnius is the oldest cathedral in the world. The original design was lost during major modifications in the 19th century. The bell tower was added a thousand years after the construction of the palace, much to the dismay of purists who long for the Romanesque tower that defined the horizon of Split for centuries.

🅐 Kraj sv Duje 5 ☏ 021 34 56 02 🕒 08.00–20.00 (summer); 08.00–12.00 & 16.00–19.00 (winter)

Peristil (Peristyle)

The main street in the palace complex is Dioklecijanova, which will lead you directly to the Peristyle, the entrance to the imperial residence. The Peristyle's southern side leads to the entrance to the imperial apartments and the eastern stairs lead up to Diocletian's mausoleum, now known as the Cathedral of St Domnius. The monumental square of the Peristyle now houses a café and serves as a popular meeting point in the area.

Spomenik Grguru Ninskom (Statue of Gregorius of Nin)

A logical starting point to view the palace is the Golden Gate, just opposite the market. The imposing statue you see is that of Grgur Ninski, or Gregorius of Nin. He was a 10th-century Croatian bishop who, as a staunch opponent of the Church and official Catholicism, incorporated Croatian language into his services rather than the traditional Latin. Notice the sheen emanating from his left big toe? Rubbing it supposedly brings good luck.

TAKING A BREAK

Bars & cafés

Bobis £ ❶ Bobis is known throughout the region as one of the finest producers of cakes, making it an institution in the world of Split desserts.

It also enjoys a great location on Riva Street. ⓐ Obala Hrvatskog Narodnog Preporoda 20 ⓣ 021 34 79 62 ⓛ 06.00–23.00

Cukarin £ ❷ All that sightseeing can be a drain on your energy level. *Cukar* is Dalmatian slang for sugar, making this the place to indulge your sweet tooth with a whole selection of tasty cakes. ⓐ Matice hrvatske 1 ⓣ 021 53 02 72 ⓛ 06.00–23.00

Teak £ ❸ If you're young, hip and like shooting the breeze or browsing a newspaper over a cup of coffee, then head for Teak. Situated on a pleasant little square, this is an excellent place to hang out. ⓐ Majstora Jurja 11 ⓣ 021 36 25 96 ⓛ 08.00–24.00 Mon–Thur, 08.00–01.00 Fri & Sat, 10.00–14.00 & 18.00–24.00 Sun

Vidilica Café £ ❹ Situated on top of Marjan Hill, this bar is the perfect place to have a drink and take some pictures of the incredible view of the city and bay spreading out beneath you. ⓐ Nazorov prilaz 1

Le Monde £££ ❺ A Croatian footballer from Split opened this combination café-bar and restaurant. It has an upstairs restaurant and a cosy garden protected by the shade of two trees that's opened in the summer. ⓐ Plinarska 6 ⓣ 021 32 22 65 ⓛ 10.00–24.00

Restaurants
Enoteka Terra ££ ❻ Offering up a bunch of Dalmatian specialities, this place would make a fine restaurant on the merits of its menu alone. However, it's the wines that make it so special. The owners, Marijana and Edi Gantar, started trading and supplying wines to local restaurants, eventually opening a restaurant and wine cellar of their own. The interior is cosy and intimate and their wine list impeccable.
ⓐ Prilaz Braće Kaliterna 6 ⓣ 021 31 48 00 ⓦ www.vinoteka.hr
ⓛ 08.00–24.00 Mon–Sat, 18.00–24.00 Sun

⬤ *Split is a great place for nightlife*

Šperun ££ ❼ The service and food are equally excellent in this tiny restaurant that is popular with tourists and locals alike. ⓐ Šperun 3 ❶ 021 34 69 99 ❶ 09.00–23.00 (summer); 09.00–23.00 Mon–Sat, closed Sun (winter)

AFTER DARK

Red Room £ ❽ This is one of the city's alternative spots, frequented by a younger crowd. Start your evening here and check out where the locals are headed. ⓐ Carrarina Poljana 4 ❶ 021 45 92 31

Gaga ££ ❾ A fancy place to have a drink before going out to one of the city's nightclubs. ⓐ Iza Luže 5 ❶ 021 34 82 57 ❶ 07.00–01.00 (summer); 07.00–23.00 (winter)

O'Hara Music Club ££ ❿ If you're in the mood for some live music, you can satisfy your cravings at this interesting music bar. Rock, blues and jazz performers do their thing on stage and there are DJ nights and other performances. ⓐ Uvala Zenta 3 ❶ 091 79 41 349 ❿ www.ohara.hr ❶ 08.00–01.00 Sun–Tues, 08.00–04.00 Wed–Sat (summer); 21.00–01.00 Sun–Tues, 21.00–04.00 Wed–Sat (winter)

Tribu Club ££ ⓫ This trendy club consistently provides the best night out on the town in Split. If you happen to be a VIP, your lounge awaits. If not, there's a pool, two bars and a terrace to keep you occupied. ⓐ Osmih Mediteranskih Igara 3 ❶ 021 38 47 45 ❶ closed winter

Hvar

Sunčani Hvar is the name Croatians have given this island – and 'sunny Hvar' certainly lives up to its name, averaging over 2,700 hours of sunshine per year (that's 7.5 hours of sun every day, for those about to reach for their calculators). Despite the many hours of sunshine, the island manages to remain green. During spring, the island smells distinctly like a herbalist's shop, with the scents of lavender, rosemary and heather wafting through the air. An aromatic Adriatic island carpeted with lovely vegetation and more sun than you can shake a stick at – it sounds pretty appealing, right? A lot of other people think so as well, which has made the island, and its capital city of the same name, an increasingly popular tourist destination during the past few years.

As with so many other places in the region, the island's popularity extends thousands of years back into history. Due to its strategic position on ancient sea routes, the Venetians, Romans, Greeks, Illyrians and even prehistoric peoples all left marks on the island that remain to this day. If you happen to arrive by car at the bar of Starigrad, try to imagine the bay as the bustling 4th-century port and capital of commerce that it once was. Today, visitors come to enjoy one of the world's elite travel destinations, an island considered by many to be one of the most beautiful in the world. They also come to see and be seen in exclusive nightclubs and to enjoy the unparalleled quality of the island's beaches.

BEACHES

Palmižana

Reachable by taxi boats from Hvar, the Pakleni islands are the best place for swimming around Hvar. It's good to keep in mind that many of the islands' beaches are naturist or swimsuit optional. Probably the best of the best around Hvar is Palmižana, the most popular. The fragrant smells that the island is famous for are prevalent here, with rosemary and heather growing in the thick forest surrounding the pebbled beach. You'll see several boats cruising by, as there's a marina in the vicinity, along with restaurants and bars.

THINGS TO SEE & DO

Fortica Spanjola (Fortress)
That steep, winding path leading north from the Old Town of Hvar leads up to the city's 16th-century fortress. It's a bit of a hike to get up there, but the fortress is the best vantage point from which to see the city and the expanse of the sea opening up in the distance. At night, the lights in town create a beautiful contrast with the dark hues of the sea.
☎ 098 56 75 41 **◐** 08.00–24.00 (summer); 09.00–21.00 (winter)
ℹ Admission charge

Hvarsko kazalište (Theatre of Hvar)
Completed in 1612, Hvar's theatre was the first in Europe to be open to the general public.
ⓐ Trg sv Stjepana

Katedrala sv Stjepana (Cathedral of St Stephen)
Certainly the most impressive building in Hvar, the Renaissance-Baroque cathedral dominates the eastern side of the square in the old town. Incidentally, the main square is the largest in all of Dalmatia at 4,500 sq m (48,440 sq ft). The majority of the construction of the cathedral was done in the 16th and 17th centuries, but the finishing touches weren't added to the interior until a century later.
ⓐ Trg sv Stjepana **☎** 021 74 12 69 **◐** 08.00–12.00, 17.00–20.00

Vrboska
This picturesque little village is located in a small inlet, with little bridges spanning a channel to connect the two sides of the city. It is home to several small churches that are some of the most treasured cultural monuments on the island. The most striking of

◆ *A narrow street in Hvar's Old Town*

these is the Fort Church. Situated on a slight rise in the town centre, this was originally a church that was fortified around 1575 to protect against attack from the Turks.

TAKING A BREAK

Bars & cafés
Lounge Bar Tabu ££ A relaxing spot with a great selection of homemade *rakija*, coffee and hot chocolate. Sit in the comfy chairs or kick back on a lounger while enjoying the smell of the sea and the well-selected jazz on the speakers. ⓐ Mala Banda, Jelsa ⓣ 098 901 02 74 ⓛ 09.00–01.00 Apr–Oct; closed winter

Sunčani Čarli ££ This place really is sunny, just like the name says. Plus, it has a prime location close to the main square and a good view of Riva, the town's main people-watching street. The terrace is great for chilling out and catching some rays. ⓐ Riva ⓣ 021 74 28 37 ⓛ 06.00–02.00 (summer); 07.00–24.00 (winter)

Villa Verde £££ After relaxing at Tabu until the early evening, head to this equally relaxed cocktail bar for an excellent selection of drinks and snacks. The pleasant music maintains the laid-back vibe. ⓐ Jelsa Bay ⓛ 18.00–02.00 (summer); closed winter

Restaurants
Bilo idro ££ Part of the charm of this restaurant lies simply in getting there. To get to the bay of Sveta Nedjelja, you need a car to pass through the tunnel that divides the island into its two halves. Once you navigate the dank and dark one-lane passage, your reward awaits. *Bilo idro* (slang for 'white sail') is housed in a curious stone building right on the water. It has a high-quality menu full of seafood favourites, but it is wine maker Zlatan Plenković's spirits that have made the white sail famous. ⓐ Sveta Nedjelja ⓣ 021 74 57 03 ⓛ 09.00–01.00 (summer); closed winter

Macondo ££ The best restaurants are sometimes tucked away in seemingly unlikely locations, and this is certainly one of them. Follow the signs from the main square to this tastefully furnished fish restaurant and enjoy some quality seafood and homemade wine. ⓐ Groda ① 021 74 28 50 ⓒ 12.00–14.00 & 18.30–24.00 Mon–Sat, 18.30–24.00 Sun (summer); closed winter

Palmižana £££ Situated in a resplendent spot on St Clement, one of the islands in the Pakleni otoci group, the ambience and the expertly prepared seafood have made this one of the most popular spots for fine dining on all of Hvar. If you're in the area, don't miss it. ⓐ Sv Klement, Palmižana ① 021 71 72 70 ⓒ 08.00–23.00 (summer); closed winter

Yakša £££ The menu in this upmarket restaurant is an imaginative mix of items you aren't likely to run into at other places. Seafood, especially

● *The historic setting of Yakša restaurant*

WILD CHERRY

Zadar's trademark product is a drink made from a bitter cherry known in Dalmatian as *maraska* (Maraschino). The cherries are quite bitter on their own but take on a better flavour as they are sweetened up with plentiful amounts of sugar. In the 16th century, experimentation in the city's monasteries led to the creation of the clear and sweet liquid that was subsequently called 'sun dew'. The tradition continues today at the Zadar Liqueur Factory, where the syrupy liqueur is produced and supposedly imbued with medicinal qualities. Either way, it tastes great after dinner on ice cream or fruit salad.

lobster, is the main attraction, but it's hard to go wrong with any of the choices offered up here. ⓐ Hektorovićeva ⓣ 091 277 07 70 ⓛ 10.00–23.00 (summer); 18.00–23.00 (winter)

AFTER DARK

Veneranda ££ All of Hvar's bars and clubs close at 02.00, except for one. Follow the mass exodus leading out of town and you'll wind up at Veneranda. Things start heating up well after midnight, with house, techno and trance spilling from the speakers, and no shortage of beautiful people to ogle. ⓐ Gojova ⓣ 021 74 57 03 ⓛ open nightly in summer

Carpe Diem £££ The crowds and prices are as big as the hype surrounding the de facto home of Hvar's A-list. If you want to rub elbows with the elite, this is the place to do it. ⓐ Riva ⓣ 021 71 72 34 ⓦ www.carpe-diem-hvar.com ⓛ 08.00–03.00

Korčula

A landscape that witnessed the unfolding of ancient Greek legends, purported home of one of the world's most famous explorers, Marco Polo, and the greenest, most interesting of the Dalmatian islands: all these claims are disputable, but as a holiday destination the island of Korčula is difficult to beat. Korčula's capital bears the same name as its mother island and is the best-preserved town in Dalmatia. That incredible level of preservation may be a result of the layout of the town, which minimises erosion by having streets curve off from one single large avenue connecting its land and sea gates.

The island has been a holiday spot for over 2,000 years, with the Greeks arriving and ultimately establishing a colony. Known as Korkyra Melaina (Black Corfu) in Greek, it also played a role in that country's mythology. Jason and the Argonauts stopped by while seeking the Golden Fleece, and it was here that Circe, the cruel enchantress, lured her victims with wine and then turned them into pigs. Korčula is also supposedly the home of another famous person, whose history is a bit more substantial than that of Jason and the Argonauts: Venetian explorer Marco Polo.

Clearly, history is an integral part of life here, existing contentedly alongside all the seductive attractions of a beautiful Adriatic island. There's some world-class sailing and windsurfing to be done, beautiful landscapes to explore and fascinating sights to see. All of which makes Korčula an intriguing destination.

BEACHES

Badija Island

The area around Korčula town can get pretty crowded, so hopping on a taxi-boat and visiting some secluded beaches might make your day. An ideal spot to try this is the Škoji Islands. Only one of them, Vrnik, is inhabited, so there are some deserted hidden beaches to discover. The best beach is probably on Badija, which is also the largest and closest island to Korčula town. The boat ride to get there takes about

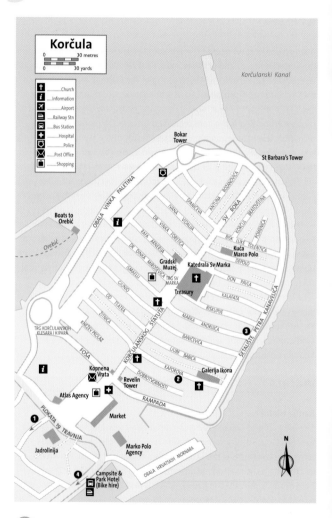

Korčula

0 — 30 metres
0 — 30 yards

†	Church
𝒊	Information
✈	Airport
▤	Railway Stn
▤	Bus Station
✚	Hospital
↻	Police
✉	Post Office
▣	Shopping

Korčulanski Kanal

Bokar Tower

St Barbara's Tower

Boats to Orebić

Orebić

OBALA VINKA PALETINA

ŠPANIĆEVA
ANTUNE ROZANOVIĆA
SV ROKA
KORČUL BRAVOĆŠTINA
POMERICA

IVANA VIDALIJA

DR VINKA TOREFICA

BISK LUKE TOLENTICA

RAFA ARNERIA

DEPOLO

DR DINKA MIROŠEVIĆA

Kuća Marco Polo

IZMAELLI

Gradski Muzej

Katedrala Sv Marka

DON PAVLA

CUNJO

TRG SV MARKA

Treasury

KALAFATA

OD TEATRA

BISKUPIJE

ŽLINCA

MARKA ANDRIJICA

KNEŽEV PROLAZ

ŠETALIŠTE PETRA KANAVELIĆA

TRG KORČULANSKIH KLESARA I KIPARA

BANIČEVICA

FOŠA

LJUBE BABIĆA

Kopnena Vrata

KAPOROVA

Galerija Ikona

DOBROTVORNOSTI

Revelin Tower

Atlas Agency

RAMPADA

Market

PLOKATA 19 TRAVNJA

Jadrolinija

Marko Polo Agency

OBALA HRVATSKIH MORNARA

N

Campsite & Park Hotel (Bike hire)

20 minutes. There's a rocky beach with clear water and some sights to visit in the area. A 14th-century Franciscan monastery stands amid the dense olive trees, pines and cypresses covering the tiny island.

Islet of Proizd

Another secluded spot can be found by doing a bit of sailing, either by taxi or via the regular boat service. The city of Vela Luka lies on the western side of the island and is significantly more laid-back than Korčula town. Regular boats make the trip from Vela Luka to Proizd three times per day. The islet is an untouched area characterised by unusually blue water, white cliffs and shade cast by dense groups of pine trees. Its beauty (and effect on visitors) has earned it the nickname 'the isle of love'.

Korčulanska Bay Beach

While you're in Korčula, this is a popular family beach just ten minutes' walk from the Old Town. The shallow water of this sandy beach makes a good swimming spot for children. There are bars nearby if you get thirsty.

Pupnatska Luka

The village of Pupnat is about 15 km (9 miles) from the town of Korčula. A bus service is available between the two towns, three or four times per day. The sandy beach caps a sharp indentation jutting into the coast, lined on both sides by hills topped with dense forest. It's certainly one of the most attractive beaches on Korčula.

THINGS TO SEE & DO

Katedrala sv Marka (Cathedral of St Mark)

On 15 August 1571, Korčula's inhabitants battled to defend their city during an invasion by the Turks. The children and women of the city gathered and prayed in front of the 'Lady of the Island' icon, housed in the town's cathedral. Suddenly, a huge storm appeared and smashed the Turkish fleet to matchsticks, saving the city. The icon is still there, housed in the most impressive building in Korčula,

⬆ *The view over Korčula and the islands beyond*

which has a stunning interior. Finally completed in the 15th century, the cathedral contains a wealth of relics and artwork, including a Tintoretto altarpiece and Annunciation as well as a Pietà and statue of St Blaise by Ivan Meštrović. Other valuable items from the cathedral are housed in the adjoining Bishop's Treasury.

ⓐ Trg sv Marka ⓣ 020 71 10 49 ⓛ 08.00–12.00 & 16.00–20.00 (summer); for services only (winter)

Palagruža Lighthouse

Ever wondered what it's like to spend your days and nights tending a lighthouse? Take a trip to the stony island of Palagruža, situated halfway between Italy and Croatia. The lighthouse was built in 1875 and stands at a height of 90 m (300 ft). This little island is rumoured to have been the home of the Greek hero Diomedes – a violent and treacherous warrior who fought goddesses and accompanied Odysseus on adventures against the Trojans.

Tours of the island can be arranged with the lighthouse keeper (yes, there really is one!). If a mere one-day visit isn't enough to satisfy your curiosity, there are apartments for rent at the base of the lighthouse. However, the island itself offers absolutely no amenities.

ⓦ www.lighthouses-croatia.com/palagruza.htm

RAISE THE BLUE FLAG

Established in 1987 by an independent, non-profit organisation called Foundation for Environmental Education (FEE), the Blue Flag is an award given to beaches and marinas based on a stringent set of criteria for both water quality and general environmental management. Marinas are judged on both the quality of their water and their services, including waste containers, access for disabled people, clean toilets and safety. Water quality is sampled in both beaches and marinas 20 times over the course of one year and beaches that receive the award are reviewed several times to ensure that quality levels remain high.

⬣ A view of Prizba on the south coast of Korčula Island

TAKING A BREAK

Bars & cafés

Fresh ££ ❶   One of Korčula's interesting watering holes. Intended to be a meeting place for travellers on the island, the 2-for-1 specials during happy hour are certainly effective on that front. They also have a menu of alcoholic smoothies and tasty wraps that you can eat on the go. And if you're in need of some reading material, there's a book exchange and foreign papers for sale. ⓐ Hrvatske Bratske Zajednice 1 ☎ 091 896 75 09 ⓦ www.igotfresh.com ⏱ 09.00–03.00 (summer); 09.00–01.00 (winter)

Restaurants

Morski Konjic ££ ❷   This traditional restaurant is known for its masterful production of all things grilled. Expect a wide range of choice meats, cooked up just the way Croatians like them. ⓐ Šetaliste Petra Kanavelića ☎ 020 71 18 78 ⏱ 08.00–01.00 (summer); closed winter

Zure ££ ❸   The people are so friendly you might find yourself insisting they join you at your table while you enjoy the excellent seafood on offer. If you do, make sure you also insist that they bring along some of their homemade pomegranate *rakija*. ⓐ Lumbarda 239, Lumbarda ☎ 020 71 20 08 ⏱ 18.00–23.00

AFTER DARK

Gaudi ££ ❹   Address, phone number or directions to this disco are unnecessary. Follow the groups of revellers heading there well after midnight. The heavyweight champion of Korčula's nightlife scene, this disco is housed in one of the oldest arsenals in the region. If you want to dance till the sun comes up, this is your opportunity. ⓐ Arsenal 3 ☎ 020 71 53 03

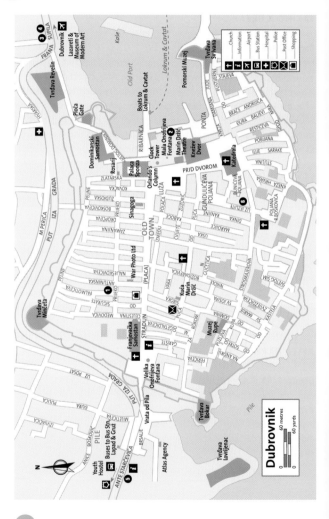

Dubrovnik

Church
Information
Airport
Bus Station
Hospital
Police
Post Office
Shopping

Lazareti & Museum of Modern Art
Dubrovnik
Tvrdava Revelin
Tvrdava Sv Ivana
Pomorski Muzej
Kaše
Old Port
Lokrum & Cavtat
Boats to Lokrum & Cavtat
Ploča Gate
RIBARNICA
PONTA
DAMJANI
PUSTIJERNE
KNEZA DAMJANI
BRAĆE ANDRIJIĆA
DURA BALJEVI
RESTIĆEVA
POBIJANA
ILIJE SARAKE
STULINA
KNEZA HRVATA
BUNIĆEVA POLJANA
POLJANA R BOŠKOVIĆA
UZ JEZUITE
Clock Tower
Mala Onofrijeva Fontana
Marin Držić Theatre
Knežev Dvor
PRID DVOROM
Katedrala
Orlando's Column
LUŽA
Palaca Sponza
Dominikanski Samostan
Rosarij
ZLATARSKA
KOVAČKA
ŽUDIOSKA
PRIJEKO
POLAČA
PRIJEKO
ZUŽORIĆ
GUNDULIĆEVA POLJANA
Sinagoga
PELINE
BOŠKOVIĆEVA
DROPČEVA
ZAMANJINA
NALJEŠKOVIĆEVA
OLD TOWN
PLACA
PUCA
CVIJETE
ŽUDIOSKA
UŠKA
MAROJICE
ĐINKA RANJINA
ULICA
STRMA
OD PUCA
BOŽIDAREVIĆA
GUČETICA
STROSMAJEROVA
SVETOG
DOMINA
NIKOLE
SV JOSIPA
SV MARIJE
KUNIĆEVA
KAŠTELA
ZVIJEZDICE
BANDUREVA
War Photo Ltd
ANTUNINSKA
PRIJEKO
Kuća Marin Držić
SIROKA
Muzej Rupe
VARA
M
GARIŠTE
Franjevacka Samostan
STRADUN
MEDOVIĆA
PALMOTIĆEVA
CELESTINA MEDOVIĆA
OD SIGURATE
Velika Onofrijeva Fontana
GETALDIĆEVA
CAKSTE
FERIĆEVA
MA ANĐELI
OD SORTE
Tvrdava Minčeta
Tvrdava Bokar
Tvrdava Lovrijenac
Pile
Vrata od Pila
Buses to Bus Stn, Lapad & Gruž
Atlas Agency
Youth Hostel
ANTE STARČEVIĆA
PUT IZA GRADA
M FERIĆA
PUT IZA GRADA
ANKE BOŠKOVIĆ
PILE
MILETIČEVA
UZ POSAT
PULCA
ĐURA
IZVIJAČICA
BRSALJE
N
0 60 metres
0 60 yards

56

Dubrovnik

Any discussion of Croatia's Dalmatian coast seems ultimately to lead to an emphatic suggestion: *go to Dubrovnik!* So what's all the fuss about? One moment spent on the city's ancient walls – viewing the glimmering sunlight playing across the limpid waters of the Adriatic – will answer that question sufficiently. Those much-celebrated walls were, of course, initially constructed for defence. In the 7th century, the region was under the control of Greek city-state Byzantium, which began to fortify the city to offer protection to the citizens of Epidaurum, which is now the modern town of Cavtat (see page 87). During the next four centuries, the city changed hands several times, but eventually became a completely independent city-state in the 14th century. Known as the Republic of Ragusa, it was famous for its skilful merchants and tradesmen and was a tiny, albeit very powerful, force, rivalling even Venice in its dominance of the region.

In 1418, the city-state abolished slavery, evidence of the forward-thinking political climate of the area at that early time. Indeed, freedom is a concept that has been exceedingly important to the citizens of Dubrovnik throughout the city's history, as evidenced by the word '*Libertas*' that adorns flags, buses and the names of two of the city's annual festivals. The walls of the city served to protect freedom and independence, and technically never fell. Dubrovnik was only conquered by the ever-wily Napoleon, who tricked his way into the city in 1806 when he reneged on his promise to respect the independence of the city. So Dubrovnik remained powerful, influential and independent until the 19th century, an achievement that still seems to imbue its citizens with a sense of pride and accomplishment. In those exquisite surroundings, they have no reason to be modest about their home. Around the Old Town, wherever you might be – either looking out of a window or taking the requisite walk around the walls – you will be struck by images of beauty, beauty, beauty.

⬥ *Local produce on sale in Dubrovnik market*

BEACHES

Banje

Check your map to find the Ploče Gate of the city walls and head there to check out the city's main public beach. Situated amid a range of fancy hotels, the visitors to this beach expect a high calibre of people-watching. The white pebbles are quite clean and you'll have a great view of the old town while you splash and swim. The shallow water makes this a good choice for children and the less aquatically adventurous members of your crew. There are so many services available on the beach, you could practically spend your entire holiday experiencing them. You can rent deckchairs and umbrellas for sunbathing, water skis for ripping around the sea and speedboats for a further adrenalin rush. Organised banana-boat and tube rides are available throughout the day. As if that weren't enough, the beach is also home to the famous Eastwest Beach Club, one of the prime party spots in the city (see page 66).

Lokrum Island

If you choose to visit Lokrum Island, make sure you bring along your bathing suit, as the tree-lined, rocky beaches around the island are some of the most popular swimming spots in Dubrovnik. There's also a small, saltwater lake connected to the sea by an inland channel known as Mrtvo more (the Dead Sea), which has a very shallow pool that is perfect for children.

Sveti Jakov

It's a 15-minute walk east of the city and a descent – and subsequent ascent – up some steep steps, but it's a small price to pay for the views of the city and pristine pebble beach just below Sveti Jakov Abbey. The beach is open to the public, and the restaurant there rents out loungers and umbrellas. Duck into the restaurant, or sit on a bar stool at the neighbouring cocktail bar to keep yourself energised.

THINGS TO SEE & DO

Dominikanski samostan i muzej (Dominican Monastery and Museum)

Built in the 14th century by the citizens of Dubrovnik, this monastery looks more like a fortress than a religious retreat. However, a beautiful cloister surrounds a peaceful courtyard with palms and orange trees. The church is large and dominated by a huge 14th-century crucifix, donated after plague had ravaged the city. It is also the burial place of the Ragusan nobility.

The brothers made sure to stop the local men's habit of eyeing up the ankles of the women climbing the stairs on their way to mass: they filled in the gaps beween the columns of the stone balustrade with mortar.

There is a museum in the east wing which displays the paintings collected by the monks. Among them is a fascinating 16th-century tryptych showing St Blaise holding a model of the city in his hand, which reveals how Dubrovnik looked prior to the devastating 1667 earthquake. ⓐ Svetog Dominika 4 ⓣ 020 42 64 72 ⓛ 09.00–18.00 Mon–Sun ⓘ Admission charge

Franjevački samostan i stara apoteka Male braće (Franciscan Monastery of the Brothers Minor and the Old Pharmacy)

The cloister of the Franciscan monastery surrounds a peaceful garden complete with orange trees and the fading remains of frescoes on the walls. The monastery is home to one of the oldest pharmacies in Europe and the third-oldest one that still operates today. There's a museum where you can view original items from the pharmacy. Outside the church on Stradun, there's a gargoyle below knee height which has been frustrating and confounding visitors for years. It's a bit of a test of strength – the goal is to stand on it facing the wall. ⓐ Placa 2 ⓣ 020 32 14 10 ⓛ 09.00–18.00 (summer); 09.00–17.00 (winter) ⓘ Admission charge

Gradske zidine (City Walls)

Two kilometres (1¼ miles) of wonderfully preserved stone enclose the city, making Dubrovnik's city walls some of the most beautiful on the

● *The fascinating Old Pharmacy*

planet. Built between the 8th and 16th centuries, the walls are up to 6 m (nearly 20 ft) thick in some places, proof of their primary function as first line of defence for the city. A walk around the entire circumference of the walls offers incredible views of the city and the sea and is absolutely essential for any visit.

🕐 08.00–19.30 (summer); 10.00–15.00 (winter) ❶ Admission charge

Katedrala (Cathedral)

Seen from any angle, the baroque cathedral cuts quite a figure on the city's skyline. Built between 1672 and 1713 by the Italian architectural duo Paolo Andreotti and Andrea Buffalini, the cathedral was erected on the site of two former churches, one of which was destroyed by an earthquake in 1667. The treasury is what makes the cathedral most famous and definitely warrants a look. Inside the golden caskets are the head and foot of St Blaise, the patron saint of Dubrovnik.

ⓐ Kneza Damjana Jude 1 ❶ 020 32 34 59 🕐 08.00–20.00 Mon–Sat, 11.00–20.00 Sun (summer); 08.00–17.30 Mon–Sat, 11.00–17.30 Sun (winter) ❶ Admission charge

Kneževdvor (Rector's Palace)

One might imagine that being rector must have been quite an illustrious position – perhaps so, but it was also a short-lived one. The rector was nominated from within the nobility for a term of one month, during which he was confined to the palace, unless he was needed in an official capacity or to celebrate a religious holiday. However, the palace wouldn't have been an altogether bad place to spend a month. A mix of Renaissance and baroque styles, it's one of the most attractive buildings in the city, now a venue for concerts and recitals in the courtyard, and the setting for a museum displaying artwork, costumes and objects from the period. You can even check out the quarters where the rector spent his short career.

ⓐ Pred dvorom 1 ❶ 020 32 14 37 🕐 09.00–18.00 Mon–Sun (summer); 09.00–14.00 Mon–Sat, closed Sun (winter) ❶ Admission charge

Lokrum Island

A 10-minute hop on the boats that leave Dubrovnik every half-hour lands you in a prime spot to enjoy some nature and tranquillity. Lokrum is a nature reserve that has peacocks (even in the trees!), a botanical garden and plenty of green to meander through. A walk through the trails zigzagging the island takes you past the natural and historical sights, including an 11th-century Benedictine monastery. Walk to the top of the hill for a great view of the island and the city, along with the star-shaped fort that the French erected there in 1806. There's a café close to the entrance and a restaurant at the site of the old monastery.

🚢 Boats depart from Dubrovnik's Old Harbour starting at 09.00 daily. The last return from the island is at 19.30 ❶ Admission charge

Palača Sponza (Sponza Palace)

This Gothic-Renaissance palace dates from the early 16th century and was actually built as a customs house. It rests on a portico of six fine columns and its interior court was a meeting-place for local merchants. Later, the building became the mint, the state treasury and a bank.

Nowadays the palace contains the state archives, which go back almost 1,000 years. There is also a memorial room honouring those who died during the nine-month siege of the city in the early 1990s. The courtyard now holds art exhibitions and concerts on occasion during the summer.

🅰 Placa Luža 🕐 09.00–13.00 & 18.00–20.00 Mon–Fri; 08.00–13.00 Sat

Stradun

Everyone keeps mentioning 'Stradun', but where is it on your map? Not to worry! Derived from the Italian word for street, *strada*, Stradun is the unofficial name for Placa, the main street that runs through Dubrovnik. With its gleaming white limestone worn smooth by the relentless shuffle of sightseers, Stradun forms the heart of the Old Town; it is lined with cafés and definitely the place to be and be seen in the evening.

⬧ *The shimmering Stradun in the Old Town is always busy*

KRAVATA – NECKTIE

It may seem ironic that an item of clothing that almost single-handedly represents an uptight, constricted lifestyle should come from passionate Mediterranean climes, but remember one thing – the Croats are kings and queens of fashion! It was back in 1635 when Croatian mercenaries from the coastal regions joined the armies in Paris to fight against the Protestants in the Thirty Years War. They wore coloured scarves around their necks, which the French military thought a wonderful idea. They were so much easier to keep clean than the lace frills that were the norm in France. Hence the new fashion was taken up with enthusiasm and rapidly spread to the rest of Europe – the word for the original wearers, Hrvat, transforming on the non-Slavic tongue to Cravat. For those of you who do not want to carry around a painful reminder of that which awaits at the end of your holidays, they are made in nice bright styles as well.

TAKING A BREAK

Bars & cafés

Talir £ ❶   Have a drink and hang out with Dubrovnik's young and arty crowd in this nicely furnished space, decked out with artworks and antique furniture. After you've finished your drink, head over to the gallery across the street for further cultural feasting, or just sit on the stone steps leading to the walls and watch the people go by.
ⓐ Atunininska ⓛ 08.00–24.00

GradsKavana ££ ❷   The location and ambience are perfect and the service is top-notch as well. In addition to the excellent coffee, they also have cakes and desserts. The rich and tasty hot chocolate goes down a treat with visitors too. Occasional live music is an added attraction.
ⓐ Pred Dvorom 1 ⓣ 020 32 10 65 ⓛ 08.00–24.00

Restaurants

Sesame ££ ❸ Modern Dalmatian and Mediterranean cuisine served up in a refined and distinctive environment. ⓐ Dante Alighiera ❶ 020 41 29 10 ⓦ www.sesame.hr ⓛ 08.00–24.00

AFTER DARK

Lazareti £ ❹ This excellent space, housed in the former quarantine house, is one of the few places in Dubrovnik where you can take in something a bit different or underground. DJs spin electronica and there are regular art exhibitions. Open till late. ⓐ Frana Supila 8 ❶ 020 32 46 33 ⓛ Fri & Sat nights

Eastwest Beach Club ££ ❺ By day, rent a lounger and work on that tan. At night, the place fills up nicely, so have a few cocktails and work on those disco-dancing moves. ⓐ Frana Supila ❶ 020 41 22 20 ⓛ 10.00–03.00 (summer); closed winter

Troubador Hard Jazz Café £££ ❻ The view of the cathedral is tough to beat, a fitting excuse for the slightly high prices. You can spend a chill night here listening to the laid-back jazz (including live sets) and soaking up the atmosphere. ⓐ Bunićeva poljana 2 ❶ 020 32 32 76 ⓛ 09.00–03.00 (summer); 09.00–24.00 (winter)

❿ *Vineyards under the mountains at Konavle*

EXCURSIONS
Out & about

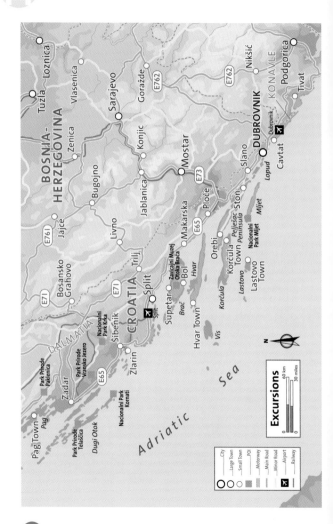

Excursions from Zadar

Dugi Otok

The island of Dugi is known as the 'long island' and is actually quite far out to sea, making it a perfect place to find some peace and quiet, even in the middle of peak tourist season. It is a paradisiacal spot full of vibrant colours and excellent beaches.

BEACHES

Saharun

Known for its remarkably clean sea, the village of Božava on the other side of the island is of particular interest for divers who come to enjoy the underwater scenery. If you prefer to stay above water, nearby Saharun Beach awaits as a fantastic day-trip destination. A vast white-sand beach stretches beautifully along the coast, and the turquoise water of the cove goes no higher than waist-level as far out as 200 m (220 yd), making it ideal for less confident swimmers. There's a snack bar offering drinks and sandwiches so you can dig in and spend the day.

THINGS TO SEE & DO

Park prirode Telašćica (Telašćica Nature Park)

No trip to Dugi Otok is complete without paying a visit to Telašćica Nature Park, an area of fascinating contrasts surrounding a 69-km (43-mile) stretch of still waters that creates one of the most beautiful bays in the Adriatic. A short walk just south of the bay is Lake Mir, a saltwater lake shrouded in mystery and steeped in legends about curious native inhabitants (who just happened to have five horns on their heads) and buried gold. The waters supposedly have curative effects – take a swim and find out for yourself. Afterwards you can just sit back and enjoy the picturesque views of the sheer cliffs that line the island. ⓦ www.telascica.hr

⬥ *A perfect place for yachting: Dugi Otok*

Park prirode Paklenica (Paklenica Nature Park)

Slicing through the rocks of the southernmost slopes of Velebit Mountain is a series of huge canyon formations, caves and rocks that just beg to be climbed. Paklenica is the common name of the two main canyons, Mala (Small) and Velika (Big) Paklenica, that rise from the sea to the highest peaks of the mountains. This transition area between sea and mountains has a collection of wondrous natural phenomena that make for an interesting visit for the casual observer and a challenging playground for hiking and climbing enthusiasts. A wide range of hikes and excursions is organised throughout the park. Located just a short distance from the sea, the park has an alpine atmosphere and makes a rewarding day trip in some of the most beautiful natural surroundings the country can offer.

THINGS TO SEE & DO

Manita Peć Cave

This 175-m (574-ft)-long cave is chock full of stalactites, stalagmites and other subterranean sights. You will need a guide to take you on the 90-minute walk to the cave and then to show you around the cave itself. Tours are organised at the reception area.

🅐 Dr F Tuđmana 14a, Starigrad Paklenica 🅣 023 35 92 02

🅦 www.paklenica.hr

Park prirode Vransko jezero
(Vransko jezero Nature Park)

A short drive south of Zadar finds you on the shores of the largest freshwater lake in Croatia, Vransko jezero (Lake Vrana). Declared a nature reserve in 1999, this body of water was of great importance in Illyrian and Roman times as an inexhaustible supply of fresh water for Zadar. Today, the park is a refuge for endangered birds – and for anglers, who come to try their hand at catching the carp, pike and catfish that populate the waters. If you'd like to try hooking some of these aquatic beauties, you need to obtain a fishing licence. Daily, monthly, weekly and yearly passes are available at most motor camps and reception desks.

⬥ *A spoonbill fishing at Vransko jezero*

Excursions from Šibenik

Nacionalni park Kornati (Kornati National Park)

An abundance of clichés could be used to describe this amazing collection of islands, but we can turn to Croatia fan George Bernard Shaw for a stirring description. He wrote about the creation of Kornati: 'On the last day of the Creation, God desired to crown His work, and thus created the Kornati Islands out of tears, stars and breath.'

Regardless of your views on creation, you can rest assured that Kornati is indeed one of the most remarkable destinations in Croatia. Sailing into the area offers unparalleled views of natural beauty, including cliffs, rock formations, and abundant flora and fauna. All of this natural splendour is preserved wonderfully, as the islands are not inhabited, giving a glimpse of nature in its untouched form.

The archipelago is divided into two groups: Lower Kornati, which is comprised of Kornat and its surrounding islands, and Upper Kornati, comprising Sit, Žut and other islands. There are two visitor reception centres that operate from June to September. One is in Žakan Harbour on Ravni Žakan island in the southeastern part of the park, and the other in Vruje Bay on Kornat Island in the northwestern part of the park. The Kornati National Park Office in Murter is open year-round. Mobile centres also cruise the waters surrounding the park at specially designated places. All of the centres offer welcome services to visitors, maps, entry tickets and general information.

There are numerous possibilities for activities in the park, including boat trips that meander through the maze of islands forming the archipelago, diving and snorkelling, or even staying with a host family that periodically lives on the islands to tend to family agricultural holdings. These activities can be arranged by the numerous tourist agencies operating either in Zadar or in the vicinity of the islands.

One of the most popular sights to view are the cliffs that stand majestically on many of the islands that form Lower Kornati. Known as *corona* (crowns), the cliffs are the result of tectonic interaction between

73

Africa and Europe, which created a collection of impressive rock walls. The highest cliff, on Klobučar island, stands at 80 m (262 ft). The cliffs are a requisite part of any boat excursion touring the islands.

🚌 There are eight buses per day from Šibenik to Murter Town on Murter Island, the first island in the archipelago and linked to the mainland by a bridge. From here, you can take a day-trip around Kornati ❶ Admission charge

TAKING A BREAK

Restaurants

Konoba Beban ££ One of the oldest restaurants in Lopatica Bay is named for the brothers who brave the seas to catch your dinner. You can assume that whatever you order will be as fresh as can be – and excellently prepared. The specialities are lamb *pod pekom* (meat is placed in a stone oven with a metal cover, hot coals on top, and cooked slowly) and *brudet* – a thick stew made with several varieties of fish. ⓐ Uvala Gujak, Murter 🕐 10.00–01.00 (summer)

◆ *Islands of the nacionalni park Kornati*

Nacionalni park Krka (Krka National Park)

A remarkable amalgamation of cliffs, rocks and waterfalls comes together to create Krka National Park, the gem of Šibenik-Knin county. The park is named for the River Krka, which originates at the foot of the nearby Donaric Mountains and eventually flows directly into the Adriatic. The primary natural attractions are the waterfalls and cascades dotted throughout the park, which range in impressiveness from the merely pleasant to the stunningly spectacular. Perhaps we need a bit of culture and history to round out all of this natural beauty. The park has these bases covered, with the Krka monastery and a small museum documenting the life of the original inhabitants of the park. Be sure to bring your camera for the plentiful photo opportunities, and also your swimsuit, so you can take a dip in the spray of the largest waterfall, Skradinski Buk. Ⓦ www.npkrka.hr

🔺 Skradinski Buk: an idyllic setting for a swim

Zlarin

The third-largest island in the Šibenik archipelago has been called many things, including the 'green island' and the 'gold island', but it is the most famous product of the island that has given it its most popular name – 'island of coral'. Red coral is supposedly imbued with several health-giving characteristics, like protecting pregnant women and unborn babies from harm and preventing blood diseases. Regardless of the legitimacy of these claims, it is the hunt for red coral that put Zlarin on the map. As far back as the 15th century, the island was an important stop on the coral trade routes frequented by Italian merchants, which helped contribute to several periods of prosperity for the island's inhabitants. Unfortunately, those times faded for the most part, but the island remains a peaceful, relaxing spot with an undiscovered, untouched vibe and friendly people that make this a particularly attractive detour.

THINGS TO SEE & DO

Muzej KUD Zlarin (Zlarin Museum)

Exhibits display a range of coral handiwork and other bits and bobs about the history of the craft that will have your coral knowledge up to scratch in no time. After viewing the exhibits, head to Zlarinka, the coral workshop connected to the museum, to see how coral jewellery is crafted using both new and traditional methods.

ⓐ Niz Bebana ☏ 022 55 37 33 🕘 09.00–21.00 (summer); closed winter

Excursions from Split

Brač

The highest peak in the Adriatic islands, Vidova gora, stands 778 m (2,552 ft) tall. Reaching the summit by car offers a view of the most famous beach in Croatia, a collection of the islands of Middle Dalmatia and a view of the south side of Brač, the island of stone. The abundant quantities of limestone, dolomite and white marble present on the island have been used in stone-working for centuries, from the temples, graves and amphitheatres of the Romans all the way to Diocletian's Palace in Split. The civilisation and culture of Brač itself was built on its foundations. You'll see houses, churches, streets, wells and towers constructed of white stone throughout the villages of the island, the same stone that adorns the White House in Washington and the

◓ *The old port of Milna*

Parliament buildings in Budapest and Vienna. That is the lasting imprint that this tiny island has made on the world.

◍ Take the frequent ferries from Split to Supetar, the main town on Brač

BEACHES

Zlatni rat

This is a beautiful beach to the west of Bol, the second largest town on Brač Island. The star of television and magazine advertisements displaying the attractiveness of Croatia's coast, the 'Golden Horn' sticks like an extended thumb into the sea, its tip changing shape according to the wind. The lively breeze blowing around the beach has made it a favourite with windsurfers, and the crystalline waters have made it popular with everyone else. Pine trees grow right to the border of the beach, offering shade for a picnic or nap. Huge, stark cliffs rise up in the background, creating one of the most beautiful settings in Croatia.

◍ There is a good bus service from Supetar south to Bol.

THINGS TO SEE & DO

Milna

Milna is a pretty port in a little bay, with narrow streets of old stone houses climbing the hill. There is a choice of cafés in the harbour.

◍ There is a daily hydrofoil from Split from July to September

Samostan Blaće (Blaće Monastery)

If you're feeling hounded by the crowds in Bol, flee to the serene surroundings of the Blaće Monastery. In the 15th century, monks made their own escape to the area to avoid the Turks who sought to conquer the island. Their monastery evolved from a simple cave dwelling to important scholastic centre and astronomical observatory. The last resident of the monastery, Nikola Miličević, was a gifted astronomer who discovered several celestial bodies. The hermitage is now a museum that houses an interesting collection, including a large library and the old

clocks that Miličević seemed to have a fondness for. It is certainly easier to visit the hermitage if you have a car, although the 12-km (7½-mile) walk can make for a pleasant outing. Keep in mind, though, that it takes about three hours each way. The route is well marked and takes you on the western road leading from Bol to a downhill footpath.

ⓐ Blaće ⓣ 091 512 93 12 ⓛ 09.00–17.00 Tue–Sun (summer); other times by arrangement

Samostan dominikanski (Dominican Monastery)

This is a 15th-century monastery in an imposing position, its lovely gardens overlooking the sea, just to the east of Bol. It houses a museum which displays a small but interesting collection of ancient treasures.

ⓐ Bol ⓛ 10.00–12.00, 17.00–20.00 Mon–Sun ❶ Admission charge

Zavičajni muzej otoka Brača (Brač Regional Museum)

The 2,000-year history of the island and the presence of its various inhabitants, including the Illyrians, Romans and Croatians, has been catalogued in the island's Regional Museum, a survey of medieval monuments, sculptures and artefacts from the Roman era. It can be found at the eastern end of Skrip village below the ruins of a 16th-century castle.

ⓐ Skrip ⓣ 021 64 63 25 ⓛ The residents of a house next door hold the key for the museum. Pay them a visit and they'll open the door for you anytime during the day. ⓝ Buses leave Supetar for Skrip in the morning and return mid-afternoon.

Zmajeva spilja (Dragon's Cave)

For thousands of years, heroic tourists have donned steel and sword and entered the fiery chasm of the Dragon's Cave, hoping to be the champion who finally frees the fair-haired princess from the clutches of the vile beast – or in their dreams they might have done. The cave was actually the home of a group of friars in the 15th century, who escaped to the remote countryside in order to pursue the saintly life. The reliefs lining the cave are a fascinating chronicle of Slavic monastic life. The

main relief features the huge dragon that made the cave famous.
ⓐ The cave is located on the south side of the island, tucked away under the cliffs overlooking the village of Murvica

TAKING A BREAK

Restaurants

Konoba Tomić ££ If it's wine you're after, this family-owned restaurant can offer up some that will definitely please your palate. They make all their wine on the premises, using an authentic winepress and traditional techniques. As for the food, everything is caught, grown and prepared by the family, right down to the vegetables from their own garden.
ⓐ Gornji Humac ⓣ 021 64 72 42 ⓦ www.konobatomic.com
ⓛ 18.00–24.00 (summer); by arrangement winter

Restaurant Palute ££ This is another family-owned restaurant that offers a whole assortment of seafood meals, but their liquid refreshment options have made them particularly well known. They make up some devilish *rakija* (brandy) in a variety of flavours – be careful, they pack a punch. They also have an outstanding wine list. ⓐ Porat 4, Supetar
ⓣ 021 63 17 30 ⓛ 08.00–23.00 (summer); 08.00–21.00 (winter)

RAKIJA

Rakija is the generic name for the huge variety of fruit and herb brandies (although just about anything can, and has been, forced through a still) that can be found in every single Croatian home, bar and restaurant. The best *rakija* is homemade: often in the villages, one person will own a still and share the firewater with the fruit growers. Naturally, all social occasions surround the beloved liquid, and guests arriving in most homes will be obliged to partake. It is claimed to be good as an aperitif and even better as a digestive. Strains particular to Croatia include *travarica*, which is made from aromatic grasses, and *kirsch* made from Maraschino cherries.

Lastovo

Dating from the 15th century, the town of Lastovo is nestled on the banks of a large natural amphitheatre that faces a rolling field of green. This is a definite departure from the norm in the Adriatic, where most cities look out onto rolling seas of watery blue. There are several other distinguishing characteristics that make Lastovo particularly special. For starters, the Croatian spoken here is slightly different from that spoken in the rest of Dalmatia. It's called the Cakavian dialect and is probably the result of the island's distance from the mainland and its prolonged relationship with the city of Dubrovnik. Then there's the architecture. As well as the elaborate interior of the parish church in the centre of town, inspect some of the houses and you'll find odd, cylindrically shaped chimneys protruding, suggestive of the minarets that adorn mosques. Yet there is no record of the island ever having come into contact with the Arab tradition. These are just a few of the little quirks that distinguish Lastovo from its Adriatic neighbours, but no doubt you'll discover others on your visit to the island and town.

Ⓝ Lastovo Island is accessible by daily ferry from Split (it calls at Hvar and Vela Luka on Korčula on the way). A connecting bus will take you to Lastovo Town

BEACHES

St Mihajlo Beach
The most popular swimming spot – a beautiful little beach called St Mihajlo – is just a short distance away from Lastovo Town.

Saplun
The beaches of Saplun, a small uninhabited island not far to the south of Lastovo, are among some of the most famous in the area. Yachts from far and wide drop anchor to enjoy the sand beaches around the island. It's a safe bet for a beautiful, relaxed day of swimming and sunbathing.

Ⓝ The Lastovo tourist office will tell you about the boat trips available.

🔺 *Lastovo sits on a steep hillside*

THINGS TO SEE & DO

Meteorological station

The meteorological station, housed in what remains of a 19th-century French fort, is perched on the large hill that overlooks Lastovo. It is rather a steep walk, but worth it because from here you can get the best view of the eastern side of Lastovo Town, the islets surrounding the island and the nearby island of Korčula.

TAKING A BREAK

Bars & cafés

Bačvara ££ A comfortable *konoba* hidden away in a passage; you'll feel like you're slipping into your local bar for a glass of wine. The interior and ambience hark back to the 19th century and the place exudes a cosy, homely kind of feel. The speciality of the house, Dalmatian cabbage, comes highly recommended, but just ask your waiter or waitress to recommend their own favourite – you won't be disappointed.
ⓐ Počivalo ⓣ 020 80 11 31 ⓛ 17.00–24.00 (summer); closed winter

Restaurants

Restaurant Triton £££ Tucked away in a bay on the north side of the island, this place offers up a whole assortment of traditional Dalmatian delights. The fresh seafood is hauled in daily by the family who own the restaurant – and is then cooked by them as well. ⓐ Zaklopatica 15
ⓣ 020 80 11 61 ⓦ www.triton.hr ⓛ 17.00–24.00 (summer); closed winter

Vis

Vis is the furthest inhabited island from the Dalmatian coast. It is mountainous with two pretty, small towns, Vis Town and Komiža. The British ruled Vis in the early 18th century, which explains why it has a cricket club. In 1944, Vis was again occupied by the British army, but now it is only tourists you will see.

Vis is famous for its red and white wines (Viški Plavac and Vugava) and also for its anchovy bread.

Ⓝ There is a daily ferry all year round from Split, which takes 2½ hours, and daily hydrofoils from Split and Hvar Town, May–Sept

THINGS TO SEE & DO

Arheološki muzej (Archaeological Museum)

Vis Island has been inhabited since Neolithic times and this museum displays its rich heritage. As well as Greek and Roman sculpture, pottery and jewellery, there are furniture and implements used by local people during the 18th and 19th centuries.

ⓐ Bateria Fortress, Šetalis Viški boj 12 ⓣ 020 71 17 29 ⓛ 09.00–13.00 & 17.00–19.00 Tues–Sun (summer); 09.00–13.00 Tues–Sun (winter)

❶ Admission charge

Modra špilja (The Blue Grotto)

To the southwest of Vis Island lies the islet of Biševo. Here you can find this enchanted grotto, which is only accessible from the sea on days when it is calm. The sunlight at its height shines through an underwater entrance to flood the cave in a wondrous blue light. Tourists have been coming here to swim in the magical waters for over a century.

Ⓝ Take an excursion from Vis Town or Komiža, or a taxi-boat from Komiža to the island. A small boat will take you on from the cave entrance.

Excursions from Dubrovnik

Cavtat

Originally a Greek colony known as Epidaurum, Cavtat gets its name from the Greek *civitas vetus* (the fugitives), a reference to the original inhabitants who fled the city to establish Dubrovnik in the 7th century. Cavtat's harbour is a picturesque one, with a tree-lined street full of shops, bars and restaurants right next to the water, a perfect spot to sit and watch the boats put-putting in and out of the harbour. Just up the hill from the harbour is Cavtat's Old Town, a small but inviting historical spot full of Gothic and Renaissance architecture. Cavtat's proximity to Dubrovnik makes it a popular day-trip destination, and it can be reached either by bus or by boat from the walled city.

BEACHES

Žal
You will find two fine shingle beaches here, approximately 1 km (½ mile) east of the centre of Cavtat.

THINGS TO SEE & DO

Mauzolej obitelji Račić (Račić Family Mausoleum)
The cemetery at the top of the hill is absolutely beautiful, offering a gorgeous view of the sea and the city spread out beneath you. The large mausoleum was designed in 1921 by sculptor Ivan Meštrović in fulfilment of the last wishes of Marija Račić, member of one of Cavtat's most famous and powerful shipping families.
🕒 10.00–12.00, 1700–1900 Mon–Sat, 10.00–12.00 Sun
❗ Admission charge

○ Cavtat's waterfront is lined with restaurants

Konavle

If you can tear yourself away from the beach, there's beautiful countryside in the area around Dubrovnik that you shouldn't miss (see photograph on page 67). Konavle is a narrow strip of land located between Cavtat and the border with Montenegro, southeast of Dubrovnik. The lush valleys and coastal areas make great places to walk and hike, but if you're feeling a bit lazy, there are plenty of places offering horse riding: choose a four-legged friend and get out there!

THINGS TO SEE & DO

Kojan Coral
Take a pleasant two-hour horseback ride through the Konavle countryside. Helmets and insurance are part of the 250-kuna fee. Newcomers to the equestrian world are welcome.
🅰 Kokoti 3 📞 020 79 88 99

TAKING A BREAK

Restaurants
Konavoski dvori ££ Servers dressed in traditional costume, a picturesque mill powered by a brook in the background, plus the excellent meat and fish dishes, have all made this a very popular dinner choice in Konavle.
🅰 Gruda, Konavle 📞 020 79 10 39 🆆 www.esculapteo.hr 🕐 12.00–24.00

Nacionalni park Mljet (Mljet National Park)

According to chapters 27 and 28 of the Book of Acts, the Apostle Paul was shipwrecked on an island en route to Rome, where he spent three months preaching the gospel and, we might conjecture, doing a bit of bathing and relaxing as well. Legend has it that the island St Paul landed

⬥ *Unspoilt Mljet Otok*

on was Mljet, the most westerly of the large Adriatic islands. If this is indeed where St Paul ended up, perhaps a bit of divine providence really was at work, for this is one of the most beautiful places one could ever hope to be. A 37 sq km (14 sq mile) island, shimmering with green, the island attracts visitors who look forward to the chance to hike, bike and swim surrounded by idyllic and peaceful scenery. Chances are you can't rely on a shipwreck to maroon you on the island, but you might wish for an extended stay just like Paul's.

❶ 020 74 40 41/58 **Ⓝ** Mljet Island can be reached by ferry from Dubrovnik **❶** You can buy an admission ticket to the park at the kiosks in either Polače or Polmen, villages which lie within the national park

THINGS TO SEE & DO

Otok sv Marije (St Mary's Island)

The National Park possesses two connected saltwater lakes, with the larger one playing host to a small island on which sits a 12th-century Benedictine monastery. It was the monks who made the lakes all salty in the first place, when they dug a channel to the sea to make sailing their boats around easier. In the 16th century, the monastery served as the centre for the Benedictine order in the Republic of Dubrovnik. Boat tickets include a pass to the island, or you can rent your own rowing boat and drop in to the monastery while cruising the lakes.

❶ 020 74 40 41/58 **Ⓝ** Boats run on demand, according to group size

▶ *A fish stall in Split market*

Food & drink

While you might be used to juggling between Indian, Mexican or Japanese cuisine as the options for a night out, this array of choices is definitely not the norm in Croatia. Generally, your choice will be between meat, seafood or pizza. That being said, different restaurants do prepare these items in individual ways, infusing the food with their own distinctive personality. And what could be better than having the chance to sample the most popular dishes in a country, prepared in the ways that locals and those in the know like them? You'll get this chance in Croatian *konoba*, which are old-fashioned traditional restaurants. Frequently they are family-owned establishments, with the entire family being involved in the process of preparing the meal.

As with many other aspects of life on the coast, the cuisine is a combination of influences from the various cultures that have called this area home at one time or another. So, you'll find Turkish, Viennese and Hungarian influences on mainland cuisine, with a strong Italian influence in coastal areas. Most restaurants on the coast offer a menu slanted towards Dalmatian specialities alongside a mix of highlights from mainland cuisine. In terms of price, restaurants tend towards the mid-price range. You won't find many that are unusually cheap or expensive.

FISH AND SEAFOOD

Fish and other seafood is generally priced according to weight, with a typical portion weighing in at 250 g (8½ oz). In some cases, the entire fish will be prepared for you. If you don't see a weight listed, this is probably what will happen. If you do choose to order an entire fish, remember that the head and tail are usually still on the fish and that you will have to bone the fish yourself. Don't be afraid to ask your waiter or waitress how to approach this if you don't know.

Coastal food is decidedly Mediterranean, enhanced by liberal doses of herbs, olive oil and garlic. The emphasis is on whatever can be caught from the sea, so expect lots of octopus, squid, lobster, shrimp and especially fish. Pasta dishes topped with seafood are a ubiquitous choice on Dalmatian menus. If you prefer to stay on land in terms of your dinner choices, a safe bet always exists – pizza. It sounds unadventurous, but the pizza throughout Croatia is actually remarkably good, and you're sure to find a pizzeria on just about every other street corner.

MEAT DISHES

Croatian menus are definitely meat-based, and the star of any menu is *cevapcici*, a sausage-like roll of minced meat and spices. They are grilled or fried and usually served in a pitta with chopped onion. Grilling meat to perfection is a high culinary art in all of Croatia. Traditional restaurants often have an open grill so you can see your meat cooking, but more upmarket restaurants will also offer grilled meats, just in a more refined setting. This emphasis on meats can make it difficult for vegetarians to find quality choices in restaurants – and they might even evoke pitying looks from waiting staff who couldn't imagine a life

🔺 *A delicious Croatian* palačinke

without meat. If you are vegetarian and are unable to find something satisfying on the menu, most restaurants will not be averse to preparing something specially.

DESSERTS

The best of all Croatia's sweets is the ice cream, which can be found piled in enormous mounds in dessert bars and ice-cream parlours. It comes in a huge array of flavours, but tends towards light and fruity. A dessert bar or ice-cream parlour will make their own ice cream from scratch with all natural ingredients. *Palačinke* (pancakes) are a very popular dessert too. There are *palačinke* shops dedicated to them, and almost any dessert bar will also have them on offer. They're essentially crepes filled with chocolate, nuts, ice cream or a wide variety of other fillings, particularly fruit.

COFFEE

Breakfast in Croatia is typically fairly straightforward and involves a pastry from the bakery and a cup of coffee. If you're dying to start your day with a heartier breakfast, you can visit a hotel that offers a buffet. If you eat or spend much time with Croatians, you'll probably find yourself consuming massive quantities of coffee. Coffee is the glue that binds the social world of Croatia together. At almost any time of day, you can see crowds of people sitting under the refuge of umbrellas in street-side cafés enjoying a cup and some conversation. You can try *kava sa šlagom* (coffee with cream) or *kava s mlijekom* (coffee with milk). Tea is available but might not live up to the standards of dedicated tea drinkers.

WINES & OTHER ALCOHOLIC DRINKS

At the beginning of a traditional Croatian meal, the diners will enjoy a touch of brandy. Croatia makes some excellent brandies, including *šljivovica* (plum) and *travarica* (herb). Depending on the flavour and alcohol content, they can be extremely potent – some taste like pure fire as they slide down your throat. Others are quite flavourful and make for a smooth aperitif. Zadar is famous for the sweet maraschino liqueur produced there, which is a cherry-based liqueur sometimes used as a dessert topping. Almost all bars will have a wide selection of imported bottled beers and at least one beer on tap. The two major beers in the country are Ožujsko and Karlovačko, which enjoy roughly equal popularity.

Croatia possesses some prime wine country, and some of the wines coming out of them are certainly top-notch, if not a bit underrated. If you happen to see someone pouring water into their wine, don't worry, it's a national custom – although wine connoisseurs find it verging on the sacrilegious given the excellence of the wines from the area. Water is used to dilute white wine and cola is used in red wine. Nearly every region in Croatia produces wine, with some makers being more distinguished than others. Wines of distinction that are worth seeking out are Dingač, Plavac, Pošip and Malvasija.

MARKETS

If ever you find yourself tired of dining out, there's usually an outdoor fruit and vegetable market in every town, at which you can grab a huge variety of fresh and healthy produce. Supermarkets have milk, ham and cheese at reasonable prices, and you can make an excellent picnic if you add just one more item: some of the superb bread turned out in Croatia's bakeries. They bake some of the tastiest bread you'll ever eat. It's always safe to choose the fluffy white bread with that deliciously flaky crust, but there are a number of other options as well.

Menu decoder

In most restaurants along the Dalmatian coast, menus are in English as well as Croatian. The majority of waiters can speak English and many also know German and Italian.

Barbuni	Red mullet	**Jaja**	Eggs
Bijeli luk	Garlic	**Janjetina**	Lamb
Bijelo vino	White wine	**Jastog**	Lobster
Boranja	Beans	**Jelovnik**	Menu
Brašno	Flour	**Jogurt**	Yoghurt
Breskva	Peach	**Juha**	Soup
Burek	Pastry stuffed with cheese/ meat	**Junetina**	Veal
		Kajsija	Apricot
Caj	Tea	**Kava**	Coffee
Cevapčići	Rolled, minced meat	**Kobasica**	Sausage
		Kruh	Bread
Čokoladu	Chocolate	**Krumpir**	Potato
Crno vino	Red wine	**Kruška**	Pear
Dagnje	Mussels	**Kuhano**	Boiled
Divlja guska	Wild goose	**Kupus**	Cabbage
Feferone	Chillies	**Lignje**	Squid
Fuži	Pasta twirls	**Limun**	Lemon
Gljive	Mushrooms	**Luk**	Onion
Govedina	Beef	**Lungići**	Pork fillet
Grašak	Peas	**Margarina**	Margarine
Grožde	Grapes	**Marmeladu**	Marmelade
Hobotnica	Octopus	**Maslaca**	Butter
Jabuka	Apple	**Maslinovo ulje**	Olive oil
Jagoda	Strawberry	**Meda**	Honey

Meso	Meat	**Rajčica**	Tomatoes
Miješano	Mixed meat	**Riba**	Fish
meso	on the grill	**Riča**	Rice
Mlijeka	Milk	**Šalša**	Tomato sauce
Mrkva	Carrot	**Sardele**	Anchovies
Na lešo	Boiled	**Šećer**	Sugar
Na roštilju	On the grill	**Sendvič**	Sandwich
Naranča	Orange	**Senf**	Mustard
Njoki	Gnocchi	**Sira**	Cheese
Oslić	Hake	**Škampe**	Shrimp
Ostrige	Oysters	**Školjke**	Shellfish
Papar	Pepper	**Skuša**	Mackerel
Pastrva	Trout	**Sladoled**	Ice cream
Patka	Duck	**Šljiva**	Plum
Patlidžan	Aubergine	**Smokva**	Fig
Pečeno	Baked	**So**	Salt
Piletina	Chicken	**Sočivo**	Lentils
Piti	Drink	**Špinat**	Spinach
Pivo	Beer	**Srnetina**	Venison
Pljeskavica	Hamburger	**Šunka**	Ham
Povrće	Vegetables	**Svinjetina**	Pork
Prženo	Fried	**Tikvica**	Courgette
Prstaci	Seafood	**Tjestenina**	Pasta
Pršut	Dried ham	**Tsikla**	Beetroot
Prženo	Fried	**Umak**	Sauce
Puretina	Turkey	**Veprovina**	Wild boar
Račun	Bill	**Voda**	Water
Rak	Crab	**Žitarice**	Cereal

97

Shopping

Pag

There are several distinctive and high-quality products produced in Croatia that can make an excellent gift or souvenir. Topping the list is Pag lace. You can find the lace in markets and shops throughout the country, but you can also head straight to the source and find it on the island itself in markets selling souvenirs and handicrafts. The same goes for the cheese famous on Pag. Simply follow the signs around the island that say *Paški sir* to grab some of the authentic item. Remember, a higher asking price usually means a better-quality product.

Expect to pay between 170 and 250 kunas for 1 kg (2 lb) of Pag cheese, and anything from 300 kunas for 15 cm (6 in) of Pag lace to 1,000 kunas for a larger piece.

Zadar

HANDICRAFTS
Pia Original paintings, ceramics. ⓐ Ulica Jadro 9 ⓣ 023 25 14 60

Studio Lik Small souvenirs like framed Pag lace or Konavle embroidery and jewellery made according to traditional standards. ⓐ Don Ive Prodana 7 ⓣ 023 31 77 66

Gradska galerija Paintings, jewellery, ceramics, bags and other accessories. ⓐ Obala Petra Krešimira IV, Biograd n/m ⓣ 023 38 59 18

MARKET
Konzum Sells Zadar's distinctive maraschino liqueur as well as wine. ⓐ Široka ulica 1 ⓣ 023 25 05 07

Šibenik

HANDICRAFTS

Mokoš Handmade jewellery. ⓐ Trg republike 6 ⓣ 022 21 93 67

◔ *The famous Pag lace is made at home*

Split

HANDICRAFTS

Đir Handmade jewellery. ⓐ Matije Ivanića 4 ☎ 021 74 22 18

Gena Men's suits made in the 19th-century Croatian tradition. Both modern and traditional designs are available and every suit is custom-made from top-quality cloth. ⓐ Ribarska 6, Trogir ☎ 021 88 43 29

Po Bota Paintings by Croatian painters. Handmade ceramics.
ⓐ Šubićeva 2 ☎ 098 21 53 79

Splite moj Dalmatian souvenirs from Croatian artisans. ⓐ Obrov 2
☎ 021 34 60 03

MARKET

Super Konzum stocks *kalipso*, a special Croatian sweet made from almonds, orange peels and figs, and SMS products – the highest-quality brand for a wide variety of Croatian products such as fig jam, olive oil and anchovies, among others. Also sells Lavanda oils and aromatic products, made from a herb. ⓐ Put Stinica 1 ☎ 021 49 04 50

Dubrovnik

HANDICRAFTS

Dubrovačka kuća Everything from paintings, wines and special sweets to postcards and small souvenirs. ⓐ Svetog Dominika 2 ☎ 020 32 20 92

Đardin Handmade jewellery adorned with semi-precious stones.
ⓐ Miha Pracata 8 ☎ 020 32 47 44

Munjčela sells hats, bags, shirts and other items embellished with handmade Konavle embroidery. ⓐ Od Puča 13 ☎ 020 32 31 84

Children

Children can expect a warm welcome, comparable to that offered in any other European country. There are playgrounds and children's areas on many of the beaches, and most hotels have some kind of children's playground or play area. A recent addition to the menus of some restaurants is a kids' selection, which is usually a chicken dish with chips and is about half the size of an adult's portion.

The clear, calm waters of the Dalmatian coast are ideal for swimming and there are sandy beaches for younger ones to play on. Many Croatian beaches are pebbly, though, so if you definitely want sand, check with the tourist office beforehand. If the kids aren't satisfied with frolicking on the beach, there are a few top-quality attractions that will definitely keep them busy for an afternoon.

The Aquarium
See a variety of aquatic exhibits and learn all about marine life.
ⓐ Kneza Damjana Jude 12, Dubrovnik ❶ 020 32 39 78

Falky Land
This place has it all for the kiddies: mini-golf, games, sport and a wide range of other activities that will have them bouncing with excitement.
ⓐ Majstora Radovana 7, Beach Borik, Zadar

Arsenal Zadar
The art exhibitions and presentations are adult fodder, but Arsenal also has an excellent children's playground. It's hard to decide which area stands out more. Good entertainment for people of all ages.
ⓐ Trg tri bunara 1 ❶ 023 25 38 33 ⓦ www.arsenalzadar.com
🕐 07.00–03.00

◔ *There are plenty of places to swim*

Sports & activities

HIKING

Paklenica Nature Park (see page 71) possesses almost 150 km (93 miles) of hiking trails, so choices abound as to the route you decide to take. The most popular trail for tourists runs from the reception area to the Paklenica Mountain Hut, a relaxed and easy walk that takes you through the Velika Paklenica canyon. The best option is to grab the map available at the reception area and plot out your own course with the assistance of the staff there.

RAFTING & KAYAKING

The Zrmanja River, east of Zadar, has rushing water, small waterfalls and picturesque canyons that make for an excellent rafting and sightseeing trip. Ami Travel ⓐ Zrinsko-Frankopanska 16 ❶ 023 30 19 20

Around 25 km (15 miles) from Split is the small town of Omiš and the source of the Cetina River. This and the mountainous terrain make it a haven for sport of all varieties, including rafting down the river. Dalmatia Rafting ⓐ Mažuranićevo šetalište 8a ❶ 021 32 16 98 ⓦ www.dalmatiarafting.com ❶ 08.00–15.00 Mon–Fri, 08.00–13.00 Sat, closed Sun

ROCK CLIMBING

The most notable climbing area in Croatia can be found in Paklenica Nature Park (see page 71). The park service can provide a full list of 400-plus climbing routes that offer challenging courses to every climber, regardless of their skill level. You can check ⓦ www.summitpost.org for information about trails, hikes and climbing in the park.

SCUBA DIVING

Croatia's varied coast has become home to a burgeoning diving industry. Most diving centres have instructors on hand that offer PADI and CMAS certification courses. If you're diving on your own, you need to get a diving card from the harbourmaster of the port, or the nearest diving centre.

Diving-Center Božava A diving school with certified instructors offering a full range of instruction, from beginner to advanced. Group discounts. ⓐ Božava, Dugi Otok ⓣ 023 31 88 91 ⓦ www.bozava.de

🔺 *Yachting is a wonderful way to see the islands and coast*

Hotel Spongiola Diving Center This diving school will help you hone or develop diving skills to prepare you for all types of diving excursions, including night diving, diving round shipwrecks and Kornati National Park diving trips.

Ⓐ Obala 1, Krapanj Ⓣ 022 34 89 00 Ⓦ www.spongiola.com

Isis Diving Centre This diving centre has comprehensive diving offers that will have you exploring the seas around Vis in no time. The company offers a selection of over 20 excursions, including trips to caves, shipwrecks and archaeological sites.

Ⓣ 021 71 36 51

WINDSURFING

Coastal towns usually have at least one company that offers windsurfing courses and rental equipment, but it's the beach near Bol on the island of Brač that has become the windsurfing capital of Croatia (see page 79). Big Blue Sport in Bol can help you master the whims of the wind; it also offers equipment rental, lessons, and can advise you on equipment and when to catch the best winds.

Ⓣ 021 63 56 14 Ⓦ www.bigbluesport.hr

YACHTING

There is definitely no better way to see the country than to hire a boat and sail the coastal waters. The Adriatic Croatia International Club (ACI) operates several of the marinas, and they are the best source of information on their location and services. They also offer the best advice on the necessary requirements for operating a boat in the country.

Ⓣ 051 27 12 88 Ⓦ www.aci-club.hr

Yacht Charter Croatia is a solid operation with 350 equipped boats, including sailing boats and luxury yachts for rent.

Ⓐ Hrvatske mornarice 1D Ⓣ 021 47 44 64 Ⓦ www.croatiacharter.com

Festivals & events

Pag

Pag Summer Festival, Pag Town
Pag's Summer Festival in August features traditional music, art exhibitions and classical music concerts, which are hosted in the town's cathedral.

Zadar

Musical Evenings in St Donat's Church, Zadar
A lovely presentation of classical music in Zadar's most beautiful setting. The festival lasts several weeks during July and August.

Saljski užanci, Dugi Otok
The town of Sali on Dugi Otok (Zadar County) hosts a three-day cultural festival featuring traditional costumes, food and music.

Zadar of Dreams – International Festival of New Theatre of Performing Arts
One of Croatia's more interesting festivals features a wide range of performance art, music and DJs over the course of several nights during July and August.

Zadar Full Moon Festival
Held on the first full-moon night in August, the River Riva is illuminated by torches and candles, and boats become markets offering traditional foods and drinks such as *rakija*, fish and seafood.

Zadar Summer Theatre Festival
The city hosts an intriguing mix of contemporary performance art from July to early August.

Šibenik

Evenings of Dalmatian Chansons, Šibenik

Šibenik hosts its own international Chanson festival in August, featuring a variety of Croatian and international performers including composers, harmony groups and soloists.

International Children's Festival, Šibenik

Šibenik's Children's Festival in June has gained international significance as an opportunity for children to actively participate in creating their own art in a variety of forms.

Split

Omiš Klape Festival

Held in Omiš, near Split, during the first three weeks of July, a festival presenting the beautiful Dalmatian art of Klape, a group *a capella* singing style.

🔺 *Folk-dancing in Pag*

Poklad Festival, Lastovo

Lastovo's Poklad Festival, which takes place in August, is one of the most extraordinary in all of Croatia. It involves an elaborate coordinated production that is repeated every year, with nearly the entire island's population participating in full folk dress.

Split Summer Festival

Held during July and early August, this is one of Croatia's most important festivals. A huge mix of performance art – ranging from theatre and ballet to concerts and opera – is presented.

Korčula

Marco Polo Festival, Korčula

Korčula celebrates being the (possible) birthplace of one of the world's most famous explorers in July, with wine, music and dancing.

Dubrovnik

Dubrovnik International Film Festival

In October, the city plays host to actors, directors and artists and presents independent films, shorts and documentaries.

Dubrovnik Summer Festival

Dubrovnik's Summer Festival has become Croatia's most celebrated cultural event, with international stars of music, dance, folklore and performance art. It lasts for around six weeks, from mid-July onwards.

Libertas Film Festival

August 2005 saw the inauguration, in Dubrovnik, of this international festival dedicated to independent and provocative film.

▶ *The 15th-century Onofrio fountain in Dubrovnik*

Preparing to go

GETTING THERE
By air
There are a number of companies that fly direct to Croatia from the UK, including several budget carriers. Prices and availability vary seasonally.

Croatia Airlines is the major operator in the country and offers flights from London Heathrow to Dubrovnik, Split, Zadar and several other destinations, both coastal and mainland. ☎ 01 487 27 27
Ⓦ www.croatiaairlines.hr

British Airways has flights from London Gatwick to Dubrovnik and Split, and from Manchester to Dubrovnik. ☎ 0870 8500 9850
Ⓦ www.britishairways.com

easyJet operates flights from London Gatwick to Split. ☎ 0871 244 2366
Ⓦ www.easyjet.com

Thomsonfly has flights from London Gatwick and Manchester to Dubrovnik and Split. ☎ 0870 1900 737 Ⓦ www.thomsonfly.com

Wizz Air offers flights from London Luton to Split. ☎ (0048) 22 351 94 99
Ⓦ www.wizzair.com

Many people are aware that air travel emits CO_2, which contributes to climate change. You may be interested in the possibility of lessening the environmental impact of your flight through the charity Climate Care, which offsets your CO_2 by funding environmental projects around the world. Visit Ⓦ www.climatecare.org

Package holidays
An all-inclusive holiday with a reputable operator booked through a high street or online travel agent or direct with the company will save you hassles and control your budget. Your operator will have a rep on hand to transfer you to the hotel and sort out any problems and will offer you various organised excursions. You can always adapt a package holiday to suit you and your family's needs, by eating out occasionally, arranging your own excursions, hiring a car for a day, etc.

TOURISM AUTHORITY

The Croatian Ministry of Tourism cooperates with the tourist ministries in several countries, along with independent travel agencies, to provide a wealth of information about the country to those interested. The following agencies can be contacted to obtain information while planning your trip.

Croatian National Tourist Office, UK @ 2 The Lanchesters, 162–164 Fulham Palace Road, London W6 9ER ☎ 020 8563 7979 📠 020 8563 2616 ✉ info@cnto.freeserve.co.uk

Croatian National Tourist Office, USA @ 350 Fifth Avenue, Suite 4003, New York 10118, USA ☎ (00 1) 212 279 8672 📠 (00 1) 212 279 8683 ✉ cntony@earthlink.net

Croatian National Tourist Office, Zagreb @ Iblerov trg 10/IV, 10000 Zagreb ☎ (00 385) 1 4556 455 📠 (00 385) 1 4557 827 ✉ info@htz.hr

BEFORE YOU LEAVE

No special inoculations are needed before entering Croatia. The tap water is completely safe to drink. A travel insurance policy is a good idea, but keep in mind that many policies exclude coverage for 'hazardous activities' such as scuba diving, rock climbing and similar, so you may have to get special cover if you are intending to take part in any such sports. EU countries have arrangements with Croatia that allow their citizens to receive health care while travelling in the country: check with your Department of Health or equivalent office to get the details (ⓦ www.dh.gov.uk). However, it is always advisable to take out a travel insurance policy before departing for Croatia.

ENTRY FORMALITIES

Citizens of Europe and North and South America may enter the country without a visa and can remain in the country for up to 90 days. All others need a visa before entering the country. It is not possible to obtain a visa at any Croatian land border. On entry, you are required to register your stay with the police, a matter taken care of by hotels, hostels and other accommodation providers. If you happen to be staying with friends, you have 24 hours to complete a small registration process at the police station. You'll need your passport to complete the process. While the police won't try to track you down should you neglect to register, taking care of that formality will save a lot of unnecessary hassle should you find yourself in trouble. Major items brought into the country, such as computers, electronic equipment, as well as boats, must be declared at customs. Doing so will guarantee that you're allowed to take them with you when you leave the country. A VAT refund is available at customs offices when you leave, so keep receipts for any items over 500 kn. Croatian art or significant cultural works must be approved for export before purchase. Further details on this process are available through the Ministry of Finance at ☎ 01 459 13 33 or ⓦ www.mfin.hr

MONEY

The currency of the country is the kuna (code HRK, though more commonly known as Kn). One kuna is divided into 100 lipa. Kuna is Croatian for marten, the little bushy-tailed animal that can be seen jumping behind the numbers on the one, two and five kuna coins. Banknotes come in denominations of 1,000, 500, 200, 100, 50, 20, 10 and 5 kunas and bear the portraits of famous people from Croatian history. Exchange offices, ATMs and banks exist in abundance in larger cities and should be easy to locate when the need arises; however, don't always rely on these in smaller island locations. Credit cards are accepted at many stores, restaurants and shops – but not all. Be sure to check in advance to see if the store accepts cards; alternatively have cash on hand, just in case.

CLIMATE

Between April and September is the prime time to visit Croatia. April may see temperatures that make it too chilly to enjoy swimming, but the weather will be clear and crisp and accommodation will be much cheaper. The months of July and August see the tourist season – and the temperatures in the area – soar to peak heights. Popular destinations such as Dubrovnik, Hvar and Zadar can become excessively crowded at this time, but the upside is that there is a bigger range of services and events available during this period to accommodate the crowds. Some maintain that September is the best time to visit the coast, as the crowds have largely dissipated and the temperature is nowhere near as hot as the peak times in summer. If you choose to visit when the temperature is a bit lower, be sure to pack both light and medium clothing in case the mercury drops. Naturally, swimming gear is necessary for any trip to the coast, and you'll want to be sufficiently protected from the sun – it can get extremely strong at times. Bring plenty of sunscreen, sunglasses and maybe even a hat to keep the rays at bay.

BAGGAGE ALLOWANCE

Croatia Airlines and easyJet offer free baggage allowance for checked luggage up to 20 kg (44 lb) on international flights for economy-class passengers, 30 kg (66 lb) for business-class passengers. Further information can be obtained on each company's website. Check restrictions on hand luggage before arriving at the airport.

⬥ A group singing traditional Dalmatian songs

During your stay

AIRPORTS

Brač – Zračna luka Brač

Brač's airport is about 32 km (20 miles) away from Supetar, the largest town on the island. It functions primarily as a take-off and landing site for charter flights, but there are some flights from commercial companies during peak season, including Croatia Airlines.

Dubrovnik – Zračna luka Ćilipi

Dubrovnik's airport is situated 20 km (12½ miles) southeast of town. There's a restaurant and café, plus other services you might find necessary, including ATM, exchanges offices, car hire and a post office. Most airlines arrange for buses to await flights, but if you don't have this luxury, you'll have to shell out 200 kn (€30) for the trip to the city centre.

Split – Zračna luka Split

The airport in Split is in Kaštela, 25 km (15½ miles) away from town. A bar operates inside the international terminal, a restaurant and lounge outside the international area, and all the other services you might need are there, including money exchange, ATM, tourist information and a post office. An army of car-hire companies operates in the airport and city buses make trips to the city at 20-minute intervals. Croatia Airlines offer a bus service to the centre. A one-way ticket costs 30 kn. If you choose to take a taxi, the trip to the centre should cost you around 200 kn (€30).

Zadar – Zračna luka Zadar

Zadar's airport is 9 km (5½ miles) away from the city in Zemunik Donji. If you need to exchange or withdraw money, there's an exchange office and ATM in the terminal. Croatia Airlines arranges buses to coincide with the flight schedule. Buses run from the airport to the main bus station in town and the quayside near the Old Town. One-way tickets are 25 kunas.

COMMUNICATIONS

If you need to use a public phone, buy a *telefonska kartica* (phone card) in post offices and kiosks. Cards cost 15, 30, 50 or 100 kunas. If you want to call internationally, pre-paid phone cards are available at kiosks and post offices, which will save you money on the cost of the call.

City codes
Dubrovnik 020
Šibenik 022
Split 021
Zadar 023
Zagreb 01

TELEPHONING CROATIA FROM ABROAD
Dial the international access code (00), 385 (Croatia's country code), the city code (without the intial 0) and the number.

TELEPHONING ABROAD
Telephoning **Australia** 00 + 61 + area code (minus the 0) + telephone number
Telephoning **New Zealand** 00 + 64 + area code (minus the 0) + telephone number
Telephoning the **Republic of Ireland** 00 + 353 + area code (minus the 0) + telephone number
Telephoning **South Africa** 00 + 27 + area code (minus the 0) + telephone number
Telephoning the **UK** 00 + 44 + area code (minus the 0) + telephone number
Telephoning the **United States** and **Canada** 00 + 1 + area code (minus the 0) + telephone number

Yellow and black *pošta* (post office) signs can be seen throughout towns and cities. The post office offers the usual services, and sometimes a few extras such as sending faxes, selling phone cards and making international calls. Post offices usually have a Western Union office inside.

The base rate to send a postcard internationally is 2.65 kunas. It costs 7.20 kunas for letters up to 10 g and 12.20 kunas for letters up to 100 g. Airmail charges are 0.80 kunas for Europe, 1.20 kunas for North America and 1.65 kunas for Australia. If you want to avoid making a trip to the post office, stamps can be purchased at kiosks. Then just drop the mail in the nearest yellow letterbox.

Internet

If you need to check your email, the easiest option is to visit an internet café. They are dotted throughout major towns and cities but can be harder to find when visiting an island. Once you're inside, the rate usually runs to about 20 kn per hour and the cafés are generally staffed by young people who will almost certainly speak English. Four- and five-star hotels have internet access in rooms and generally have business centres with high-speed internet connections that charge a fee if you're not a guest of the hotel. If you want to access the net wirelessly using your laptop, T-Mobile operates HotSpots in Split, Zadar, Dubrovnik and in several ACI marinas. For a complete list of HotSpot locations, visit Ⓦ www.t-mobile.hr/hotspot and click the *lokacije* tab. For instructions on how to connect to the service, visit Ⓦ www.t-mobile.hr

CUSTOMS

There are no special customs that need to be observed along the Dalmatian coast, but given the turbulent decades that Croatia and the surrounding region have experienced recently, discussion of the war – and the issues that gave rise to it – is something that is best avoided. The war had lasting repercussions that are still felt in many families and communities, so, to be on the safe side, avoid touching on the subject.

DRESS CODES

Naturist and topless bathing are a part of the daily routine on many of Croatia's beaches. Naturist beaches will be marked with 'FKK' (short for the German *Freikörperkultur*), but keep in mind that there are many unofficial spots where it is acceptable for women to sunbathe topless. See Ⓦ www.cronatur.com for further information.

When visiting nightclubs and discos, it is best to err on the snazzy side in terms of dress to avoid looking a bit out of place when all those sharply dressed Croatians start arriving.

If you visit a church, it is respectful (and required) to refrain from wearing sleeveless shirts and short skirts.

ELECTRICITY

Electricity is 220 volts/50 hertz and uses the standard European two-pin plug. Visitors from the UK will need an adaptor.

EMERGENCIES

The emergency numbers are universal throughout the country. The level of English spoken in Croatia is generally very high, so you can feel relatively certain that you'll be able to communicate with someone in case of an emergency. Pharmacies are plentiful – look for a green cross accompanied by the word *ljekarna* (pharmacy).

◉ *Unusual street sign*

EMERGENCY NUMBERS
Police 92   **Fire Department** 93
Ambulance 94   **Coastguard** 9155
Road Assistance 987

Dubrovnik
General Hospital @ Roka Mišetića bb 📞 020 43 17 77 🕐 24 hours

Šibenik
Hospital @ Stjepana Radića 83 📞 022 21 24 99 🕐 24 hours

Split
Hospital @ Spinčićeva 1 📞 021 55 61 11 🕐 24 hours

Zadar
Emergency @ Ivana Mažuranića 28 📞 023 23 98 00 🕐 24 hours
Hospital @ Bože Peričića 5 📞 023 31 56 77 🕐 24 hours

EMERGENCY PHRASES

Help!	Upomoć!	*U-po-motch!*
Stop!	Stop!	*Sto-p!*
Call a doctor!	Pozovite liječnika!	*Po-zo-vi-te li-yech-ni-ka!*
Call an ambulance!	Pozovite hitnu pomoć!	*Po-zo-vi-te hit-nu po-motch!*
Call the police!	Pozovite policiju!	*Po-zo-vi-te po-li-tsi-yu!*
Call the fire brigade!	Pozovite vatrogasce!	*Po-zo-vi-te va-tro-gas-sie!*
Where's the nearest hospital?	Gdje je najbliža bolnica?	*Gdj-e je naj-bli-cza bo-lni-ca?*

UK CONSULATES

If you find yourself in legal trouble, you have the right to contact your country's consular official. They can provide advice and assist you in obtaining legal help from an English-speaking lawyer. However, they will not pay for the service.

Split
Honorary Consul ⓐ Obala Hrvatskog narodnog preporoda 10
ⓣ 021 34 14 64

Dubrovnik
Honorary Consul ⓐ Bunićeva Poljana 3, 20000 Dubrovnik ⓣ 020 324 597

GETTING AROUND
Car

The costs associated with travelling through Croatia by car can be high. Petrol is fairly expensive and there are tolls on all major highways. If you plan to take your car on any islands, reservations are a must and it can be quite expensive. However, seeing Croatia by car can enhance your total travel experience, as it affords you freedom and mobility that you would otherwise not have if you depended exclusively upon public transport.

The law recently changed to make the legal limit for alcohol when driving a straightforward 0.0 per cent – no alcohol whatsoever – and the police really do enforce it. Speed is a problem on the curvy mountainous roads around the coast, so you'll probably encounter some speed traps while you're driving. Stay under the speed limit and you won't have a problem. The limit in cities and urban areas is 50 km/h (30 mph) unless marked differently; 80 km/h (50 mph) on secondary roads and 130 km/h (80 mph) on motorways. If you're caught speeding, fines can be charged on the spot and you'll be asked to show your driver's licence, registration documents and your car insurance. Most insurance companies in the UK automatically add Croatia to their list of covered countries, but it is always better to check before your trip. You can check with the Croatian Automobile Club for advice by calling ⓣ 01 455 44 33.

Car hire

The major car-hire companies operate in Croatia and there are also independent agencies. The major advantage of using an international chain is that they offer a one-way service, so you can start in one location and drop the car off in another. Independent agencies sometimes offer this service but operate fewer offices. You must be 21 years of age to rent a car, and some companies require you to have had your licence for at least two years. Third-party liability insurance is included in the agreement, but you will want to make sure that you have full insurance, known as the Collision Damage Waiver (CDW). See your rental agreement for exclusions to the CDW policy. In the event of an accident, you should immediately call the police to ensure a police report is filed; otherwise, the CDW is not applicable and you are responsible for the full amount of damage to the car.

Argus Car Hire Ⓦ www.argusrentals.com
Budget Rent-a-Car Ⓦ www.budget.hr
Europcar Ⓦ www.europcar.com
Hertz Ⓦ www.hertz.hr
Sixt Ⓦ www.e-sixt.com

Public transport

The Croatian bus service is excellent and is generally the preferred way to travel. At larger bus stations, you'll need to purchase your ticket inside the station. It's a good idea to reserve a seat in advance, especially during peak season. If you're on a trip lasting more than a few hours, there will probably be one or two ten-minute stops for refreshment at a petrol station along the way. Most routes will include several stops to pick up passengers along the way. There are also night buses available. For city buses, tickets can be purchased directly from the driver and usually average about 8 kn. Tickets can be purchased at a discounted rate at kiosks. Tickets need to be validated when you enter the bus. Look for a small box with a rectangular slot near the bottom and insert the ticket with the arrow pointing towards the box until you hear the sound of the machine stamping the ticket.

Travelling by train can prove to be more comfortable than by bus, but the Croatian rail system does not service many destinations on the coast. The only railway for coastal towns runs between Zadar, Šibenik and Split. It is important to note that there is no train service to Dubrovnik. Despite these inconveniences, a recent 'high-speed' addition to the service has cut the travel time between Zagreb and Split to about 6½ hours. When travelling by train, there are two options, either 'express' or 'passenger'. Express trains have first- and second-class seating that can be reserved in advance, and smoking and non-smoking sections, along with sleeper cars for the train from Zagreb to Split. Passenger trains offer second-class seating and you cannot reserve a seat. For more details and timetable information, visit Ⓦ www.hznet.hr. At the time of writing, passengers are not able to book online.

Ferry

Jadrolinija has a virtual monopoly on ferry services in Croatia. All inhabited islands are connected to the mainland and a coastal ferry plies the waters from Rijeka to Dubrovnik. If you're planning to do some island hopping, verify in advance that ferry services exist between your planned destinations. Many ferries from islands bring workers to the mainland, and so leave the island very early and return late afternoon, so it is extremely important to check the schedule carefully to ensure you're not stranded. Most routes operate year-round, although some routes stop during the off season. There is always room for passengers, but if you have a car, it's important to reserve in advance. Tickets are available from the ticket collector, who will generally go window-to-window to sell tickets.

There are some shuttle ferries on which it is impossible to reserve a space. The two major destinations that use shuttle services are Korčula Island and the towns of Drvenik and Sućuraj on Hvar Island. If you wish to use these ferries, arrive early, park your car in the queue and buy a ticket. Some boats are modern and offer a whole variety of services, while others are a bit more run-down. If you're taking a particularly long ferry trip, bring food and something to drink just to be on the safe side.

◔ A ferry leaving Hvar harbour

HEALTH, SAFETY & CRIME

The Dalmatian coast is an exceedingly safe place, although visitors should always be aware that random street crime can happen at any time. Most visitors will feel secure walking the streets, even at night, but it's obviously a good idea to keep your eyes on your belongings at all times. *Policija* (police) can generally be relied on to be helpful to tourists. They do make occasional checks of identity documents, so have some form of identification on you at all times.

MEDIA

Croatian television is full of foreign programming, much of it in English with Croatian subtitles. Some kiosks carry international newspapers in English, and major bookstores will usually have an English section, although the quality of these varies greatly. Imported books can be rather expensive, so it's definitely advisable to bring your own reading material.

OPENING HOURS

Standard office hours are from 08.00 to 16.00. Banks are open 08.00–20.00 on weekdays and 08.00–12.00 on Saturdays. Post offices are a main hub for day-to-day chores like paying bills, and so keep longer hours than most businesses. They are open from Monday to Saturday, 07.00–21.00. Many shops and stores are closed on Sunday, but the ones that are open will generally close their doors at 13.00. Many businesses have seasonal hours, so be aware that some places might be closed entirely or have different winter hours.

RELIGION

Previously, one could find a robust mix of religions in Croatia, including Roman Catholic, Christian Orthodox and Muslim. Following the recent war, however, the balance of the population changed, with a fall in the number of Christian Orthodox Serbs: the 2001 Census reported 88 per cent of the population as Catholic and 4.5 per cent as Christian Orthodox.

TIME DIFFERENCES

Croatia is in the Central European Time Zone (GMT plus one hour, GMT plus two hours during daylight saving time, March–October).

Add or subtract the given number of hours to or from Croatian time to get the time in each country.

Australia +8 hours
New Zealand +10 hours
United Kingdom −1 hour
United States Eastern Standard Time −6 hours
United States Pacific Standard Time −9 hours

TIPPING

Tipping is at your discretion, but you can show appreciation for good service with a 10 per cent gratuity.

TOILETS

If you're in need, follow the WC sign. Toilets are generally well kept and cost 2–3 kunas for that luxury. Alternatively you can head to a café or restaurant, but you will need to order a drink or something to eat in order to justify admission to their facilities. *Muški* designates the men's room and *ženski* is women's.

TRAVELLERS WITH DISABILITIES

More attention is being paid to the needs of disabled travellers along the Dalmatian coast, although services are still not quite up to the standard you might expect to find in other Western countries. Most major hotels have access for disabled people, and virtually all parking areas and garages will have some kind of access. The best way to get up-to-date information is to call or visit the local tourist board in each city.

SPOT THE BEST BEACHES

Now we help you to get more from your holiday before you've even unpacked your sun cream. Each great pocket guide covers everything your chosen resort has to offer, meaning you'll have so much more to tell the folks back home. We've included everything from the best bars, clubs and restaurants to family-friendly attractions and of course all of those sun-drenched beaches.

HOTSPOTS
ALGARVE

HOTSPOTS
MOROCCO

Titles in the series include:
Algarve, Bulgaria, Corfu, Corsica, Costa Blanca, Costa Brava & Costa Dorada, Costa del Sol & Costa de Almeria, Côte D'Azur, Crete, Croatia, Cuba, Cyprus, Dominican Republic, Egypt, Fuerteventura, Gran Canaria, Guernsey, Ibiza, Ionian Islands, Jersey, Lanzarote, Mallorca, Malta, Menorca, Mexico, Morocco, Orlando, Rhodes & Kos, Tenerife, Tunisia and Turkey.

ACKNOWLEDGEMENTS

The publishers would like to thank the following individuals and organisations for providing their copyright photographs for this book:

Plava Ponistra: all photographs except Pictures Colour Library pages 1, 67, 87; Robert Harding pages 78, 122.

Copy editor: Penny Isaac
Proofreader: Jan McCann

Send your thoughts to
books@thomascook.com

- Found a beach bar, peaceful stretch of sand or must-see sight that we don't feature?

- Like to tip us off about any information that needs a little updating?

- Want to tell us what you love about this handy little guidebook and more importantly how we can make it even handier?

Then here's your chance to tell all! Send us ideas, discoveries and recommendations today and then look out for your valuable input in the next edition of this title. And, as an extra 'thank you' from Thomas Cook Publishing, you'll be automatically entered into our exciting prize draw.

Send an email to the above address or write to:
HotSpots Project Editor, Thomas Cook Publishing, PO Box 227, Unit 18, Coningsby Road, Peterborough PE3 8SB, UK